THE ALMOND FLOWERS
AND OTHER STORIES

ANIL GHARAI (1957–2014) was a writer from Midnapore, West Bengal. He has authored seventy-four books and many of his stories and novels focus on the life of the marginalised in rural Bengal. For his outstanding work in Bangla prose fiction, he has received awards such as Sanskriti Puraskar, Bharat Excellency Award, Tarasankar Puraskar, Sopan Sahitya Puraskar, Bankim Puraskar and many others. His major works are *Nunbari, Dourbogarar Upakhyan, Ananta Draghima* and *Parijan o Onyanno Golpo*.

INDRANIL ACHARYA is Professor and Head of the Department of English, Vidyasagar University, West Bengal. He has authored, edited, and translated several books and is the Chief Editor of *Janajati Darpan*, an international multilingual series on indigenous studies.

ANURADHA SEN is a translator and teacher based in Kharagpur, West Bengal. She graduated from the University of Calcutta and completed her Masters from Vidyasagar University. She translates Dalit literature from Bangla to English.

ARUN PRAMANIK is Assistant Professor of English at Gour Mahavidyalaya, affiliated to the University of Gour Banga, Malda, West Bengal. His essays and translations have been published in various academic journals and edited volumes.

SAYANTAN DASGUPTA teaches Comparative Literature at Jadavpur University and is the co-ordinator of the Centre for Translation of Indian Literatures. He is also a member of Advisory Board (English), Sahitya Akademi.

Anil Gharai has long been writing about the marginalised and the downtrodden people. He writes about the voiceless section of the society. He is a writer of commitment and integrity. I am glad that some of his stories are coming out in English. I am sure that these stories will introduce him to a wide readership. I wish him success. He has always been one of my favourite authors.

Mahasweta Devi

THE ALMOND FLOWERS
AND OTHER STORIES

ANIL GHARAI

Edited by

INDRANIL ACHARYA

Translated from the original Bengali by

ANURADHA SEN and ARUN PRAMANIK

Foreword by

SAYANTAN DASGUPTA

Orient BlackSwan

THE ALMOND FLOWERS AND OTHER STORIES

ORIENT BLACKSWAN PRIVATE LIMITED

Registered Office
3-6-752 Himayatnagar, Hyderabad 500 029, Telangana, India
e-mail: centraloffice@orientblackswan.com

Other Offices
Bengaluru, Chennai, Guwahati, Hyderabad, Kolkata,
Mumbai, New Delhi, Noida, Patna

First published 2022

ISBN 978-93-5442-317-8

042851

Typeset in
Adobe Jenson Pro 12/14
by Le Studio Graphique, Gurgaon

Printed in India at
Replika Press Pvt. Ltd.

Published by
Orient Blackswan Private Limited
3-6-752 Himayatnagar, Hyderabad 500 029, Telangana, India
e-mail: info@orientblackswan.com

Dedicated to

Srimati Sarbani Gharai

Wife of Late Anil Gharai

Contents

Foreword

Dalit literature has been a visible category of Indian literature for many decades now. Writers of Dalit literature from languages such as Gujarati, Marathi and Tamil have by now become popular even in language spaces outside their own, thanks to translation.

However, it is only much more recently that the Dalit literary movement in Bangla has gathered steam. The widespread idea that Bengal had not seen a Dalit movement and there was no Dalit literature worth its name in Bangla has now been well and truly put to rest. While many of these writers have been writing for several decades it is again over the last decade or so and again thanks, not in a small measure, to translation that this has happened. Powerful works written in Bangla by writers such as Kalyani Thakur, Manju Bala, Manohar Mouli Biswas, Manoranjan Byapari and many others have today become more visible. These writers have today been recognised as being among the leaders of Bangla Dalit writing today. We are well on our way to seeing Bangla Dalit writing as an important category within Bangla literature.

A number of Bangla Dalit literary works have been translated into various languages, particularly into English, over the last few years. This is again significant as far as the growing visibility and accessibility of Bangla Dalit literature is concerned. Anil Gharai is one of the most important writers from the oeuvre of Bangla Dalit literature. This anthology of thirteen very powerful short stories by Gharai is a timely effort and promises to make this writer accessible to a larger section of readers as well as to augment our understanding of the nuances and diversities within Dalit literature.

While the Dalit autobiography has probably enjoyed the greatest visibility and popularity among scholars and critics, many critics have also pointed to the fact that fiction from the Dalit literary canon imbibes a large quantum of autobiographical elements. In that way, Dalit literary fiction negotiates between life and literature in a unique way, and it is therefore being increasingly seen today as a mode and genre that can foster a better understanding of our contemporary Indian realities.

Gharai's short stories definitely fulfill this promise. The stories translated for this volume focus on characters from the grassroots of Indian society. These stories explore the underside of modern India. It is instructive to note that Gharai's protagonists include the vagrant slum dweller ('Bindiya'), the unlettered and unemployed youth who leaves his ancestral home and travels to new places in search of work ('The Eternal Bond'), the ill-paid village midwife struggling to look after her ailing son ('German's Mother'), and the poor village chowkidar ('The Chowkidar').

People who make a meal by scavenging for leftovers at village feasts and people who compete with dogs in their struggle for survival are characters we encounter in this writer's works. That is the brutal, dehumanised reality that Anil Gharai depicts in his fiction. His stories focus on the most deprived and the oppressed and give a voice to the voiceless, a visibility to the plight of those rendered invisible in the national imaginary.

Another important theme is violence, which manifests itself in many different forms in Gharai's fiction. Sometimes violence figures as revenge as in the story 'Bindiya,' in which, the protagonist finds no other way to save herself, her dignity and her family. Again, in 'The Eternal Bond,' violence is seen as a manifestation of power in the case of the jealous contractor who covets Basmati, while she harbours feelings for Sudama, the labourer. Sexual violence recurs as a theme in other stories as well. For instance, in 'The Almond Flowers' Gharai uses the almond tree as a powerful symbol of the burgeoning love between the protagonist Habhati and the Sepoybabu, and its final fate.

Gharai deals poignantly with the father–son relationship in at least two stories in this anthology—'The Chowkidar' and 'The Gangman'. These two stories could not have been more different, but both focus on this relationship in terms of a specific socio-economic context—that of the deprived, the downtrodden and the voiceless.

Perhaps one of the most powerful short stories in this collection is 'German's Mother', which foregrounds a heart-rending conflict for the protagonist. Faced with the opportunity of exacting revenge on the man who is responsible for all her misfortune and sorrow, the woman is beset by her strong sense of ethics and professional duty as the village midwife who is trusted by those in their most vulnerable state. The conflict between her desire to avenge her husband's murder and the desire to espouse her natural and essential sense of humanism is portrayed acutely and poignantly by the writer here. It is stories like this that make this collection an engrossing and powerful read.

Sayantan Dasgupta

Preface

> 'Exploitation is a double-edged sword—it comes as much from outside as from within the tribal society. So I avoid pointing fingers. My job is to highlight what I see.'
>
> Anil Gharai

In modern Indian Dalit literature, autobiography remains the most powerful genre for the assertion of Dalit consciousness. Sharankumar Limbale's *Akkarmashi,* written at the age of twenty-six, created a huge furore in the world of mainstream Marathi literature. His book reveals how his mother was bartered away to three landlords for bare survival. This autobiography resonates with the conflict one can identify in African-American literature of the late twentieth century. The authentic quest for truth in Dalit autobiographies exposes a harsh and naked reality that can never be discovered in the writings of eminent non-Dalit writers like Premchand, Manto, Bibhutibhushan Bandyopadhyay, Tarasankar Bandyopadhyay, Manik Bandyopadhyay, Mahasweta Devi and others, despite their acute and often powerful portrayals of the dispossessed and those living on the extreme margins of society and humanity. *Sadgati, Hnasuli Bnaker Upakatha, Aranyak, Padma Nadir Majhi, Chotti Mundar Teer*—all these classic creations on subaltern reality are essentially third-person narratives. They fail to register the fierce protest against Brahminical social order in the first person. In this regard, Marathi Dalit authors have played a pioneering role. Daya Pawar's *Achhut*, Lakshman Mane's *Upara*, Prahlad Kamble's *Ayetwan Chopakshi*, Shantabai Kamble's and Baby Kamble's autobiographies have formed a unique oeuvre of protest literature that represents a hitherto-suppressed subaltern experience narrated most passionately. A trenchant critic of Premchand, Omprakash Valmiki, in his book *Joothan*, has also challenged the deep-rooted system of exploitation in the name of untouchability. Of course, Dalit writings in Marathi, Gujarati, Kannada and other languages of south India have assumed the dimension of a people's movement.

In this context, Anil Gharai's fiction in Bengali may be closely analysed. He did not produce any autobiographical writing as other Dalit authors in other regions of the country did. But his novels and short stories have questioned the representation of Dalits in mainstream Bengali literature. Along with Gharai, Kapil Krishna Thakur, Jatin Bala, Nalini Bera, Afsar Ahmed, Achintya Biswas, Shyamal Kumar Pramanik and many other Dalit authors have challenged the literary Brahminism in Bengal. Their literary outputs resonate with the protest tradition of African-American literature on the one hand, and on the other, with the incipient literary creations of Dalit poets in the earliest *Charyapada* texts of Bengal—the first utterance of Dalit identity vis-à-vis a Bengali identity.

II

In the context of Bengal, caste issues have always been overlooked as retrogressive in a progressive Marxist state. Unfortunately, a long rule of thirty-four years failed to properly address the finer aspects of caste-based discrimination in Bengal. Rather, Marxist insistence on class struggle and the utopian dream of a dictatorship of the proletariat completely engaged the intellectual universe of the 'Bhadralok' Communist ideologues in the state. Anil Gharai's stories, such as 'Parijan', 'Kuth', 'Bilbhat', 'Tikli', 'Loo', 'Rakto', 'Urangara' and many others capture the subaltern reality of this so-called progressive Marxist state with great literary prowess. Gharai ruthlessly exposes the hypocritical ideologies of the progressive, liberal political philosophers. An echo of Dr Ambedkar's conflict with Marxist ideology can also be clearly heard in his narratives. Unfortunately, Dalit authors like Anil Gharai inhabit a narrow space in literature whereas there is a growing market for mainstream urban/metropolitan popular fiction, often influenced by Western literary traditions, that easily engages the attention of the common readers.

III

Sincerity and authenticity in literature has been a topic of discussion since the days of British Romanticism. Authors such as Tarasankar, Manik, Bibhutibhushan, Samaresh Basu, Satinath Bhaduri, Banaphool of the yesteryears and Bhagirath Mishra, Jhoreswar Chattopadhyay, Swapnamoy Chakraborty and others of the present generation do not have the direct lived experience of pain and suffering and humiliation of a Dalit existence. From that point of view, Advaita Malla Barman was the pioneer in presenting an authentic Dalit experience in *Titas Ekti Nadir Naam*. Anil Gharai's fiction spans a wide geographical area covering various pockets of coastal Bengal and Odisha and the forests of south-west Bengal, Odisha and Jharkhand. In a way, his writings are a very authentic documentation of Dalit voices in the eastern part of the nation—a record that matches the breadth of vision found only in Mahasweta Devi.

The Almond Flowers and Other Stories brings together thirteen short stories about different marginalised sections of our society. The stories portray how communities deemed as 'untouchable' and tribal groups are marginalised in a society governed by money and muscle power. The stories render visible a hitherto invisible section of society—the poorest of the poor. Within the brief span of each narrative piece, we see tragic events in the accursed lives of the downtrodden play out. Thus, we discover significant micronarratives of various subaltern groups in the garb of fiction. Stories like 'Bindiya', 'The Palanquin', 'The Eternal Bond' and 'The Plunderer' have a unique appeal of their own. To conclude, this anthology is an authentic representation of the lived realities of the unrepresented subaltern of the twenty-first century, and it questions the development paradigm by focusing exclusively on the heart of underdevelopment.

IV

Translation is a challenging task, and the act of translation is in many ways an act of 'parallel creation'. Translation bridges the gap between two different cultures—that of the source language and the target language. For the translation of this volume, there arose the need for a rich vocabulary to present to the readers the meaning, style and rhythm of the original stories without any distortion as it was essential that the translation remained faithful to the original.

The translators carried out this arduous task with utmost care. For words or phrases that have no equivalent in the target language, the translation required careful research to understand why a particular word or metaphor was used in a particular context and its role, and then ensuring that the meaning and tone of the original is conveyed accurately in the translated text. Translating Gharai's stories requires exceptional sensitivity towards and understanding of nuance in language as he often paints word pictures in his stories, which have complex themes such as the interplay of love and lust in 'The Eternal Bond',the struggle for survival in 'Hunger', the courage of characters like Habhati and Bindiya against the lechery of men, or the changing interpersonal relationships in 'The Gangman' to name a few. The verbal acrobatics in Gharai's writing such as his use of pithy sentences, audacious metaphors, peculiar inflections of regional dialects to convey authenticity and the sometimes lyrical, almost dreamlike quality of his prose—though thoroughly enjoyable to Bengali readers—make the task of translation even more challenging. The translators Anuradha Sen and Arun Pramanik have been very careful to safeguard the original beauty of the author's characteristic word plays while also keeping anglophone readers in mind.

We hope that readers will find this collection of Gharai's stories in translation as intriguing and absorbing as they are in the original.

Acknowledgements

We are profoundly indebted to the following individuals for their direct and indirect contribution to the making of this volume.

Sarbani Gharai, wife of late Anil Gharai and noted Bangla Dalit author, for her kind permission to translate the thirteen selected short stories of Anil Gharai included in this anthology.

Sudhangshu Shekhar Dey and Subhankar Dey of Dey's Publishing, Kolkata, for bringing the literature of Anil Gharai to the limelight and making his works popular among Bangla readers.

Anuradha Sen and Arun Pramanik for translating these stories of Anil Gharai flawlessly into English and making them accessible to a global readership.

We also thank leading Anil Gharai scholars like Susnata Jana, Sunil Maji, Kinnor Ray, Tapan Bandyopadhyay, Jhoreswar Chattopadhyay, Bhagirath Mishra, Adhir Biswas, Swapnamoy Chakraborty, Amar Mitra, Mangala Prasad Roy, Debashis Chanda, Palash Biswas, Saheli Mitra, and Saibal Chatterjee, among many others.

We acknowledge Suman Ray, Arindam Dasgupta and his associates for providing excellent technical support to make the manuscript error-free.

Finally, we pay our sincere homage to the late Anil Gharai and hope that his blessings will make this literary endeavour a resounding success.

BINDIYA

Bindiya did not think even in her wildest dreams that she would be caught red-handed. Bhanumati, her mother, had warned her about this place, which was still new to them. Bindiya was scared. But fear would not get them a square meal. Or a single meal. She remembered Ramlal's words: "Protect your self-respect. Without it, nothing matters."

That was easy to preach but difficult to practise. She did not want to leave the shelter and comfort of her hut. But what could she do? Her mother had been released from the hospital. After so many days she had seen a smile on her mother's face. Holding Bindiya's hand she had said, "Do not worry about me, daughter. Yamraj will not touch me." But he had touched Bhanu ten years back. Bindiya was only eight then. She clearly remembered her mother's condition as she shook Bhanu, asking him to wake up. Ramlal had tried to comfort her. Bindiya did not remember his words but her mother's mournful figure had left an indelible mark upon her mind—something that the passage of time would never wipe out.

The sun had just begun its westward journey across the pale blue dome, scattering its rays in the grey of dawn as the rainclouds gathered one by one. The land turned darker than the sky, a cold wind blew and the scattered clouds came close together as if to burst upon the earth with all their fury. They did burst. The rain came down in torrents, flooding the land and the meadows. To save themselves from the fury of the rain and the storm the vagrant dwellers had taken shelter in the railway shed, abandoning their poor huts. The huts would be difficult to save, thought old Ramlal. His calculation about the rain was wrong. He never thought it would set in so soon. Ramlal and his group stayed in the small shacks close to the railway station, with dense jungles at the back. The faint rumbling that shook the earth always woke up Ramlal. Unwinding the heavy cotton wrapper that covered him like a shroud, and shivering in the chill air, he would take up his lantern and go out to see if all was well. Day in and day out his people wandered about; some practised a variety of trades and occupations. They were hardworking not only for want of money but because of the life and vitality that was in them. If anyone wanted to sell amulets and the like, it was fine; old Ramlal had no objection. Bindiya sold red, blue, yellow and green plastic flowers. Her mother Bhanumati made beautiful flower vases.

Ever since Bhanumati fell ill, Bindiya's anxiety and responsibility had increased. How could one remain calm when even ration was so difficult to get? How long would Ramlal cater to their needs? Moreover, this brewed resentment among the members of the group as well. Some pulled long faces while others looked away. Fulki advised Bindiya to find some work, adding that she would soon start looking like a worm-eaten creature if she remained idle.

Bindiya had neither the desire nor the ways and means to remain idle. After her father Bhanu's death, Bindiya and her mother were plunged in grief. But life had to go on and a living had to be made, and that responsibility now fell on them. Both mother and daughter tried to earn their livelihood by selling plastic flowers and vases. They did not make much, but it was honest labour, and what little they took home at the end of the day was precious. The rich and the cultured bought their colourful plastic flowers that seemed to sparkle with Bindiya's bright and ardent sprit. The flower vases held the buyers in wonder. Seeing the vases, Ramlal, too, remarked in surprise, "They are first-class. Even a thousand rupees is less for them."

Jhatulal sold medicines made from herbs and the like. His wife Lachmi sold bead necklaces. Red, yellow, green and blue beads neatly and beautifully strung by Lachmi herself.

Everybody in the group did some work or the other. "Without work how can you survive? How can the group survive?" Ramlal often said. Yet he knew too well that if circumstances forced them to leave a place, they would perhaps never return. The old man spoke the truth when he said, "The vagrant has no fixed address. No one can ever know our whereabouts. We stay where we please."

So it was in the course of their wanderings that Bindiya left her childhood far behind. Standing at the threshold of youth, Bindiya loved to dream of better days and better times. Bhanumati now looked pale and common, without light or beauty. She worked in silence, unconcerned about how she appeared to others. Jhatulal, a middle-aged man, was more anxious about his trade; otherwise he didn't have much to worry about. Lachmi, his wife, was about thirty-five.

Ramlal, the oldest member of this group, was like the banyan tree. He gave shade and shelter to the members who he said were like his children. Broad and strong despite his seventy-odd years, he was always afraid and apprehensive of the people and the places where they halted.

With the break of dawn there was a bustle in every hut. Everybody was up and ready to set out with their professional equipment to look for customers. They left after listening carefully to Ramlal's instructions, feeling secure that their children and their meagre belongings were in safe custody. To

Bhanumati in convalescence, nothing mattered. She remained in the hut preoccupied with herself.

"No," she said. She did not want the chapatis and the mouth-watering spicy food Bindiya cooked for her. Not even the pickles. Couldn't she have some rice and the meat of a broody hen? Bindiya had promised her.

However in the morning, Bindiya was at a loss. The rains which came down in torrents had taken everyone by surprise. So nearly the entire group sought shelter in the abandoned railway shed with their belongings. There was no other way out. It was much wiser to save themselves than to remain in the waterlogged huts and die. Bindiya sat with a heavy heart watching the rain. The level of water rose as its surface mirrored the sky and the clouds but the rain did not stop. The rainy season brought untold misery upon the vagrant dwellers. They had nothing to do. Ramlal was busy narrating stories to the children. His storytelling never failed to cast a spell on his young listeners. His language was lucid, easy-flowing and intimate. Standing a few paces away, Bindiya listened to the fantastic story, her mind searching the shelter of her long-lost past when she too used to nestle close to Ramlal. Today of all days she could not afford this luxury. She had to tend to the needs of her ailing mother. Ramlal had told her again and again not to go out. "This *samaj* is not good. The people who creep about in this sordid samaj are not good. Their life is marked by obscenity and immorality."

Bindiya knew that Ramlal was not concocting stories. Her mother was not allowed to go out when she was young. Back then, her father Bhanu was the earning member. Bhanumati and others like her remained in the shacks doing their jobs—trying, forever trying, to save themselves from the piercing looks of the men. But in vain. Most dangerous were the khaki-uniformed ones. They were coarse and vulgar, and their eyes narrowed at the very sight of young women. With their warm complexion, vigorous, slender bodies, rough-hewn faces and deep brown eyes full of life, the women were desired by them. These men drew in a deep breath, licked their dry lips and ordered the women to report to the local police station reminding them of the dire consequences of failing to follow their orders. The women went, only to return the next morning. Back in the shacks, the men would sit and wait. Time crawled by like years. When the women returned with signs of repeated brutal assault, they looked uglier than flowers that have been crushed mercilessly. Their muffled sobs spoke of their loss as each woman sat slumped in dejection trying to shrink within herself. Their heart-rending sobs would wake Bindiya up. Often she had sat in the darkness and listened as she had never before listened to anything; Ramlal tore his hair in desperation and her father had along with the others readied themselves for a fight. That was all. They knew all too well the result of this unequal fight, and so they endured what they could not cure. Cut off from the natural spontaneous rhythms of life, these people trudged on with their children and women. Their women were taller than the women of the *babughar* and their dark, deep eyes complemented their warm complexion perfectly.

Oh god! Did they deserve such beauty? Beauty that made even the most indifferent stop and look once. Such questions disturbed Bindiya for she failed to get answers. In the darkness of the night, her eyes lit up like fireflies while drops of sweat made their way along the curves of her breasts and fell on her navel, jerking her back to her present. Bindiya never wanted such a life but the Almighty had been too generous in her case.

Ramlal knew very well the gnawing grief in the hearts of these women. Anything that spelt danger to his group put him instantly on his guard. In the darkness of the night, he would flee to some other place. This vagrant life had lost all its charm for Bindiya. Whatever pleasure this life could have offered her was snatched away by the glitter and glamour of the stable, settled life—the life, not the people though. Strong and ruthless with their hunger for flesh, they had robbed the virginity and chastity of so many Munnis and Lachmis and Bhanumatis.

The mirror was a taboo for Bindiya. Bhanumati expressed her displeasure explicitly, "Foolish girl, how will you save yourself if you deck yourself thus?" But what could Bindiya do? She loved to wear yellow-tinselled *ghagra-chunni*.

Ramlal did not stop her. He said in a loud voice that gold always shone by itself. Bindiya was a beautiful, high-spirited girl. Even the dogs looked at her with wide eyes. Bhanumati too looked at her own flesh and blood in wonder and amazement, and a deep sense of sorrow welled up in her.

The group of about twenty people gathered under the railway shed and stared vacantly at the rain. There was nothing to do. They sat in groups, their hilarious tones of gossip breaking the monotony of the incessant rain.

Only Jhatulal went out once for tea leaves. He needed a glass of tea on this rainy day to shake off his inertia. Bindiya too went out. She did not wait for the rain to stop. From the depth of Bhanumati's anguished soul softly welled up the mournful cry—

"Do not go, child. Do not go."

Nothing could stop Bindiya. Gathering her wrapper close around her, she stumbled on, sometimes along the railway tracks, sometimes across the meadows. Generally nobody went outdoors in such weather. After all, it was an unknown place.

Bindiya walked confidently, determined to get what she had promised. She had not done anything for her mother and she did not want to miss this opportunity. She would sell the flowers and the money would come in handy. But oh, the rains! Finding no customers, Bindiya thought of going to the local shops. Surely the shopkeepers would appreciate the handmade flowers.

The shopkeepers did appreciate—not the flowers, but Bindiya the budding flower. However angry and sad she might have felt, she could not summon enough courage to stand up against them.

Then she hit upon an idea. The sahibs of the railway colony had refined taste. They loved flowers. Each and every house had a flower garden. Bindiya entered the colony with the aim of selling flowers. But there was no one to buy any.

Bindiya's determination started breaking down. Though the rain had stopped, the current of her thoughts did not. She summoned all her strength. She would not return empty-handed. She looked up to chalk out her next move and was surprised to find the sun shining splendidly and the sunlit clouds sailing across the sky. The rays of the sun washed over the meadows and marshes. There was an air of wholesomeness everywhere—something that was not there the previous night. Bindiya laughed at her fears. It fled with the wind as the sun and the clouds conspired with each other. For the first time ever, Bindiya emerged a victor in the battle of life. She saw the hen, drowsy and languid, by the fence. Bindiya was ready. She caught the hen by its neck and lifted it clear off the ground.

Quickly but skillfully, she wrung its neck. The hen flapped its wings once... twice... and then it was all over.

Bindiya put it inside the folds of her long skirt. As she started walking, she felt the warmth of another body. Her face turned white, her eyes widened and her breath was inaudible. It was as if it was not the hen but a young man who had clutched her soft belly. She stood still. Waves of desire flooded her and she tried to breathe. The muscles of her stomach relaxed and so did the girdle. The throttled hen fell upon her feet. Bindiya was caught red-handed. The next moment Bindiya was pushed into the chicken run. The helpless girl tried to save herself from repeated attacks and blows as clouds of pain and humiliation spread over her face and bitter remarks were thrust into her ears.

"Such an innocent face, but so wicked."

"She must be taught a lesson."

"Let's take her to the police station. She will speak the truth when she is flogged."

The word 'police' darkened her vision. All the vagrant dwellers were not thieves. Ramlal's order in this matter was clear. If anybody robbed or stole from others, he would turn them out.

"I will go without a square meal but never will I rob others."

Bindiya wondered with a heavy heart how she would face the affectionate Ramlal. Her mother would writhe in pain and shame. She would lament that Bindiya ought to have perished in the womb.

Bindiya was conscious of a searing pain down her back. She could not ask pardon for what she had done. And because there was no pardon, she did not want to be taken to the police station. To the vagrant dwellers the police were the most dreaded. Bindiya remembered the case of Munni—Ramlal's only grand-daughter. She was as beautiful as a fairy, and her beauty had paved the way for her tragic end. She was called to the police station one evening. Ramlal had gone along. He was asked to wait and then after an hour ordered to leave. Munni would return after she had completed her work, he was told.

Much before dawn Munni had returned. She could hardly walk. Bhanumati had helped her in. They had given her only twenty rupees. She was told to leave immediately else they would set fire to their huts. Bhanumati had tried to console her.

"So many things happen in life, child. Learn to compromise. There is no other way out. We have no shelter, no place to stay—only the road full of thorns and briars. If you are pricked by a thorn, wipe off your blood." But Munni could not reconcile herself to her lot. She hung herself from the big tree just opposite their hut. The lust for flesh had taken its final toll. Bindiya had never thought that such would be the ultimate end. She had shuddered and stood rooted to the spot. Ramlal had only said, "It is unfortunate that Munni could not even attain the final beatitude. How could she when men turn into beasts?"

Since then Bindiya had been scared of the police. Yet, the very nature of their work made it impossible for them to stay away. She had killed the broody hen and so there was simply no question of mercy. Tears rolled down her cheeks. With folded hands she pleaded but she failed to soften the hard hearts of the people. She was abused and accused of theft. They said, "These people are dangerous and cold-blooded. During the day they come to our colony under the pretext of selling goods. Actually they make a note of everything. Then they return to rob and to kill."

The policeman came before Bindiya was taken to the police station. The middle-aged pot-bellied policeman's joy knew no bounds when he saw her. He said he knew her and the rest of her clan. He had been to their huts to claim his commission. Holding his baton in one hand, he walked with measured steps towards Bindiya.

"Let me take care of her," he said. He caught Bindiya's hand in a firm grip and eyed her shrewdly.

"So, what do you have to say? Nothing? Eh! Come to the police station. I'll clip your wings in no time. Once and for all."

"Let me go, please. I will never do it again." But Bindiya's words fell on deaf ears. Walking a few paces, the policeman said, "What will you give me if I let you go?"

"I will give you flowers to decorate your rooms."

"Flowers, plastic flowers! What would I need them for? Especially when you are with me—a beautiful, budding flower!"

Bindiya smiled. A sad, mournful smile.

"You like flowers?"

"Of course I do. And that is why you are with me."

"If it is so then let me go. I will come to you at dusk. I'll make you happy."

"Is that a promise?" Delight and joy flooded his face as he barked, "Now don't forget. If you do not come, I'll see to it that you starve."

Bindiya could not swallow even a mouthful of rice that day. The day was fleeting and dusk would set in very soon. She looked at Ramlal who sat huddled in one corner of the hut thinking. Bindiya knew that to Ramlal, rain meant despair and untold sufferings.

A troubled Bhanumati looked at her daughter. Usually cheerful and lively, Bindiya appeared quiet and withdrawn.

"Why are you so quiet? What is troubling you? Tell me," said Bhanumati.

"I have a headache."

"Come to me, child. I will apply a balm."

Removing her wrapper Bindiya went and sat close to her mother. Tears welled up in the corners of her eyes. Her face was clouded with anxiety. Bhanumati's eyes noted all these and her heart was filled with a brooding fear. Suddenly Bindiya said aloud, "This place is getting on my nerves. I'll be very happy to leave."

"There is nothing new in any place under the sun. Everywhere it is the same. There is nothing good or bad for us, the vagrant dwellers," Ramlal sighed. He continued after a pause, "The police here do not demand much. Whatever we give, they accept without a word. This place suits everybody. What is the harm if we stay here for a few more days?"

Bindiya said nothing. She was not in a state to say anything. She was sweating, trying hard to suppress the violent agitation within her. Bhanumati looked at her intently.

But it was too much for the helpless girl to endure. Looking at her mother she said, "Have you forgotten Munni? I cannot forget her, mother."

Bhanumati was panic-stricken. She looked at her daughter once again and understood the reason for Bindiya's silence. She could read the sorrow on her pale young face. But what could she do? She came out in the open with Bindiya.

"What is it? Tell me," Bhanumati said with an unmistaken urgency that voiced her fear and sorrow.

"I have to go to the police station this evening. Sepoybabu has told me repeatedly. If I don't go, they will ransack our huts."

Bindiya started dressing though there was still time. Bhanumati's hand did not tremble as she helped her daughter to dress. Her child was growing up and from now on she would have to fend for herself. But how much longer could Bhanumati shelter her? Bhanumati's hand shook as she tried to put a red bindi on Bindiya's forehead. Tears ran down her cheeks and Bindiya whispered in pain.

"Mother!"

Bhanumati said, "Do you want to say something?"

"If I do not return... if like Munni...?" Bindiya could not complete her sentence. Her voice choked and she looked at her mother with anxious eyes. Bhanumati seemed to her so cruel and hard-hearted. How could she send her daughter? She knew the consequences. What could be more degrading?

Old Ramlal guessed that something was wrong. It was like the lull before a storm. Bhanumati's face narrated the fearful episode of the yesteryears. Ramlal looked around. There was a stony silence on his face. He spoke out in fury, "Bindiya will not go anywhere. You go."

"Me?" Bhanumati asked pointing a finger at herself and her pale, worn-out appearance. "What do I have? Whatever I had is all gone. Will those out there, restless with their lust and desire, take the wax without the honey?"

"Even then, you go."

"Why will they accept me? What if they ask me about Bindiya?"

"Tell them that the unfortunate girl has fled in fear. Many run away. It is nothing new."

"And if they don't believe me?"

"Then bring them here. Tell them to search."

"If you are caught?"

"It is not easy to catch Ramlal."

Bhanumati went when dusk was setting in. But she could not pacify the sepoy. His voice shook with anger as he said, "I will teach her a lesson. I will squeeze every drop of her youthful beauty." The sepoy did not wait till dawn. With his men he reached the meadows where the vagrant dwellers sat trembling in fear inside their huts. He searched the huts and turned them inside out. Then seething with wrath, he began throwing out their belongings one by one. The men beat up old Ramlal who took the merciless beating in his stride but never once opened his mouth.

Bindiya saw everything from the treetop. Old Ramlal had instructed her to go up there. Bindiya did not want to but Ramlal had reasoned with her. He had tried to make her understand the importance of chastity in the life of a woman. Bindiya had sat up there watching every move. She was to stay there till Bhanumati returned.

But Bindiya did not stay there. She could not hide herself in the dense branches when Ramlal was being beaten up. She walked up to them—her hips swaying, her lips moist and slightly parted.

Bhanumati looked like she had seen a ghost. Old Ramlal could not utter a word. Bindiya looked at them with wide eyes as she drew in a deep breath and said carelessly, "Come, Babu, let's go. Since I have given you my word, I will go. The *Banjaras* do not go back on their words."

On both sides of the railway tracks darkness had set in. Along the dark path Bindiya walked on. She remembered her mother as she was in the days of her youth—beautiful and delicate as a flower. Yet people had trampled upon her because she grew by the roadside. Bindiya did not like this. Her eternal and unusual desire was to be loved. She walked for some time and then called out to the sepoy who was instantly on his guard.

"What now?"

"Can I ask you something?"

"What is it?"

"You are not married, are you?"

"No. And that is why I have come to you."

"You like me then?"

"Y...e...s."

"Then take me home, Babu. Marry me. I want to have a family, a home of my own." Tears started rolling down her cheeks yet she continued, "Our life is full of ups and downs, it is not stable. My mother could not save herself. People like you used her as a commodity. I do not want that. Please give me a shelter."

"That is not possible." The policeman looked at her with anger, "People will laugh at me. I will be shunned by everyone if I marry you. You are meant for roadside pleasure only."

Bindiya was stunned by his cruelty. After sometime she said, "Then go back. You will not be able to endure Bindiya's sting."

"I know how to deal with the sting as well as the poison."

"Then don't blame me afterwards."

There was darkness everywhere. An overpowering darkness that could make one blind. The policeman's face burnt like a brand and his warm breath washed over Bindiya who was absolutely cold. Her blood was boiling and she saw the policeman as the symbol of persecution to which she and others like her had been subjected. Munni had said goodbye to the cruel world. But she, Bindiya, would not give up the struggle so easily.

At long last, after what seemed an eternity, it was all over. Bindiya pulled out the knife from her corset. What Munni could not do, what her mother could not do, Bindiya did perfectly. The silence of the tranquil night was shattered as the policeman rolled over crying out in pain. There was blood running down his thighs—something that only the Munnis and the Lachmis and others like them had been adorned with.

Bindiya ran back to her mother panting. Bhanumati could not understand anything. She did not see what Bindiya held in her hands as red drops of blood fell and covered the ground.

Looking at Bindiya who had a frenzied look in her eyes, Bhanumati said, "It is a sin to hang yourself. Come to me, child. I don't want to walk through this world without you." Bindiya stopped dead. Then in a faint whisper she said, "I want to live, mother. Life is to be lived, and to be lived fully and joyfully. I want to live as a flower adorning the roadside."

Translated by Anuradha Sen

THE ETERNAL BOND

The glaring sun shone on the long range of barren and rough mountains. The land too was barren like the rocks. The spade produced only harsh sounds—sounds that intensified the despair and disappointment of the farmers. Sudama Kunkal left his village far behind and stood at the foot of the mountains. He looked as far as his eyes could see and he saw the singed village and his entire being seemed to sink into an abysmal void. He turned his eyes away and then looked at himself in surprise. With his bag on his shoulder and the *ukha,* he was ready to set out. His string of ankle bells was in the bag. At the first opportunity he got he would take it out, tie it and then as the bow of the ukha rose and fell with the rhythm of the song, Sudama would sing and dance and attract listeners.

Sudama's village was far away from where he was standing. It spread around and along the stream, shaded by dense jungles. The neighbouring village knew of Sudama's love for music. Even if nobody wished to listen to the songs he sang, he knew the gentle winds and the waters of the river would carry his songs far and wide. It did not matter whether the crowd applauded or not. For just a bowlful of rice beer he would sing at least ten songs. The driver of the local bus would stop for Sudama even though he had no money to pay the fare. He would sing to pay the dues. People were very fond of this unlettered, romantic youth.

Old Kadma, Sudama's mother, told him again and again that he should not leave his ancestral village and set out for some alien land. "Only two mouths to feed, my son. We will manage somehow."

Sudama Kunkal knew it was not that simple. The hot summer months wiped away any little hope that he had nurtured. He had no work. The people at the local market no longer listened in rapt attention to his songs, which were lost in the loud blare of the speakers. The modern film songs were in no way less responsible. These songs attracted the village folk more than Sudama's humble songs woven around the familiar themes of loss and pain. For three days Sudama had been going around the fair singing in a high-pitched tone. Even then, he could not collect even two kilos of rice. His whole body was covered with prickly heat. An enraged Sudama felt that there was no end to his troubles. In desperation he cursed the evil star under which he was born. The chowkidar had told him that it was high time Sudama began paying him a commission. He demanded a full rupee, adding that the people could not shop in peace because of Sudama. He was sure that Sudama had links with the pickpockets who roamed about in the fair.

Sudama shuddered. It was a sin to even listen to such words. Since that day, Sudama had not set foot at the Wednesday fair. He was too scared of slander and defamation.

"I am an artist, not a beggar," Sudama said, "And the ukha is my life." He had tried many a time to make the gentlemen understand this simple truth. The blind and the lame earned their living by begging. But his ukha was not an alms dish. It produced music which was a balm for broken hearts. He would play the ukha in the soft stillness of the night and sing his newly-composed songs, and his mother would listen to them. But never would he beg.

Sudama walked along the Ranchi-Chaibasha road with such thoughts in mind. Under a hot sky and a blazing sun, the land was throwing up dust, which pricked his eyes like needles. There were only two or three customers at Basmati's local shop. A few dogs lay under the peepal tree, panting in the heat. Basmati beckoned to Sudama with a smile on her lips and a twinkle in her eyes. Her soft, tender face was full of compassion and warmth. Looking at Basmati, no one would ever think that she had griefs gnawing at her heart like worms.

Sudama looked around before he walked towards the shop. Rice beer was not what he needed now. Basmati however was too insistent. Couldn't Ukhababu sit at her shop for a moment? "If talented men like you step into my shop, my heart feels so light," Basmati said in a deep voice.

Sudama sat on the wooden bench, swinging his legs and throwing inquisitive glances around. Suddenly his eyes fell on Basmati's shapely form. Clad in a striped saree and her hair oiled and combed, she seemed bewitching. Sudama sat there in the hot summer noon oblivious of his surroundings—he was drawn towards her by her dark provocative eyes and her lotus-like shoulders drooping in the noonday sun. A green bindi on her forehead would have looked so beautiful, he thought. She wore a beaded necklace that ran along the curve of her heavy breasts and touched her waist. Her lips seemed to be darker than the dark liquor that she served.

Sudama turned his eyes away in guilt and shame. It was not decent to observe someone so minutely. Basmati was unaware of Sudama's turmoil. She came forward with a bowl of rice beer in her hands. With a smile she said, "Take it, babu. I made it especially for you. Then sing a song, will you? It's been such a long time since I heard you sing. Yet, I clearly remember the song that you sang at the cock fight. What a melodious voice you have, babu! Even the ukha loses its identity and becomes one with you in your song."

Sudama sipped his rice beer, "I did not know you were so fond of music and song. Really, who would want to listen to music in this scorching heat?"

Basmati did not reply. She turned her eyes towards the brown land that lay like a creature paralysed, its back covered with dried, blistered skin. The faint smell of the scorched land reached her nostrils. The road lay bare and empty in the afternoon. The bus from Chaibasha had left long back for Chakradharpur. Those who had alighted had gone their way. Sitting face to face with Sudama, Basmati said, "Are you leaving? Why are you carrying your bag? I have never seen you with it before."

Sudama finished the last dregs of the rice beer and looked at her, "Yes. If I remain here, I will die. I am going to Medinipur. One can find work there. These summer months I will work. I do not mind working as a field hand. Kunu Sangi promised me a job there. He is supposed to come here today. But he still has not."

"You have fallen into Kunu Sangi's trap then. Be careful, he is not a nice man."

Sudama burst out laughing. Picking up his ukha, he said, "No one can harm me as long as I have the ukha with me. Even pain and sorrow cannot touch me."

What Basmati understood heaven alone knew. She looked at Sudama with tears in her eyes and said in a low voice, "I would have gone with you had I known. I do not like to sit by the roadside selling rice beer. People throw dirty glances at me. I feel very scared."

"I don't understand you," said Sudama, surprised. "There is still time if you wish to come. The truck for Chakradharpur will come again after seven days. From there we will go to Medinipur. This time about fifty of us are going."

With a sigh Basmati turned away.

Sudama found it difficult to move. The rice beer had brought a drowsy numbness over him. Basmati's shop had just a flimsy awning held together by poles that could break any moment. Basmati paid no attention to it. Chased out by her husband and branded a witch, Basmati was shunned by one and all. Those who came to her shop were loaded with dirty intentions. Yet, Basmati remained calm; the light in her eyes dispelled all darkness.

A customer came covered in sweat, carrying an axe on his shoulder. Sitting on the low bench, he eyed Basmati with eyes full of lust. Basmati gave him some rice beer and looked intently at Sudama. Then she said what was never to be said, "Compose a song about me, Ukhababu. This wretched life has many stories to narrate."

Before Basmati could finish, the truck crowded with people arrived. Sudama was not prepared for this. From the truck came indistinct sounds of murmuring. He looked around for Kunu Sangi as going to Medinipur without him would be useless. He did not have the address of the brick field.

When Sudama was looking around for Kunu Sangi, Basmati came and stood in front of him. Heaving a sigh she said, "Are you going by this truck? My goodness! So many people!"

"There are no jobs here. People set out for unknown distant lands for one square meal. If a man wishes to save his family, he has to leave behind the shelter and comfort of his home to earn a livelihood."

The light went out from Basmati's eyes. She walked back to her shop with downcast eyes. Kunu Sangi jumped down from the seat beside the driver's and looked at Sudama doubtfully. In a stern voice he said, "Who is that girl? How do you know her?"

Sudama could not think of a reply. He stared at Kunu Sangi vacantly and remembered his warning: the previous night, Kunu had told him not to look at any girl. If he did so, Kunu would pull out his eyes. "In the brick field, men and women work together. It is like a family. I do not wish to see any misdemeanour there." Sudama had told Kunu that he loved to spend his time in music and song. When would he have the time to look at girls?

Whatever work was assigned to him he would do and never would he disobey Kunu.

The train from Chakradharpur was to leave at 4 p.m. It was quite late. Still, Kunu drank three bowls of rice beer and gave Basmati two rupees extra.

Kunu said, "Your rice beer is very good, I'll remember the taste for a long time." He looked at Basmati with lovesick eyes. Before leaving he said, "We will meet again. Today I have no more time to spare. I will return in seven days and drink rice beer to my heart's content."

Basmati refused the extra two rupees. She said with hesitation, "This is extra. I will not take this. I will take just the price of the rice beer."

"You will be the loser if you do so." Kunu Sangi looked at her with shrewd eyes, "No one will be able to pay the price of your rice beer. It cannot be paid. Nobody can name the price for the rice beer that has the touch of your hands."

Kunu Sangi had a way with words. Basmati softened and a strange look came upon her face. Kunu Sangi left the place in style. He wiped his moustache and without even a backward glance went and sat beside the driver. The truck sped towards Chakradharpur. Before they crossed the river, Kunu Sangi came and stood in the middle of the crowd like one about to deliver a lecture. In a loud voice he said, "Chakradharpur is a town and the police are always roaming about. I will leave you there for some time. If you see me, do not show in any way that you know me. Buy your tickets, board the train. I will find you before Kharagpur. But be careful. Do not say anything that will lead us into trouble. If they catch me they will not show any mercy. I know that the people of this district should not be encouraged to go work as labourers anywhere outside. If our case becomes known, none of us will be able to go. I hope you understand what I mean. So try not to dig your own grave."

Sudama knew that Kunu Sangi spoke the truth. This practice of enticing field hands had raised strong protest from all quarters.

The lure of a job and everything that came with it took the simple folk to far-off lands. At the end, their limbs were cut off and sold. This is wrong, Sudama thought. One day he would compose a song on this burning problem. His job was not only to sing but also to bring about an awakening.

That whole night about fifty labourers took rest at the Kharagpur railway platform. Kunu enjoyed a full meal of rice and mutton at a nearby hotel. The labourers received a loaf of bread and a banana each, just enough to satisfy their hunger. Soon they fell asleep. But Sudama could not sleep. He gazed in surprise at the piece of bread. Then as he settled down to sing, he suddenly remembered Basmati's enchanting eyes. It seemed to him that she was standing close by with a bowl of rice beer in her hands, her eyes full of ardour. What was it that Basmati wanted to say? That she was branded a witch and chased out by her husband. What else?

With a sigh, Sudama took up his ukha and drew the bow across the string of the instrument. A plaintive tune flowed out into the silent night while all life seemed to have slowed down. And Sudama had a perception of a silence beyond silence. It made him feel that all things around him sang the same song which he could hear distinctly—not with his ears but with his mind and spirit. The harsh light of the platform mingled and merged with the soothing light of the moon that stood quiet and serene in the sky. The winds forgot to whisper. The cacophony of sounds melted into each other. The world listened awestruck to the song that poured out from the depths of Sudama's being. The song that Basmati wanted to sing but could not.

Kunu Sangi came to Sudama. He wanted to know if it was a passionate longing that found expression in his song. "How will you stay without her? If you neglect your duties my reputation will be at stake."

Sudama raised his eyes to meet Kunu's, "You need not worry about me. Even if I do not do anything to add to your prestige, I will do nothing to harm it. The man who sings to the music of the ukha can never be a thief or a robber." Then Sudama stepped out into the open to admire the golden glory of the moon. Everything seemed so beautiful—the heap of clayey soil, the bricks lying in blocks and pairs here and there, the shrieks and cries and the peals of laughter of the workers working in the brick fields.

"Yes, it is beautiful," said Sudama. Beyond the brick field and the green rice fields and as far as the eyes could see was the vast expanse of clear sky and the distant horizon where the green and brown of the land touched the blue of the sky. Tall trees surrounded the field where neat furrows stood in close embrace. The gentle winds aroused in him feelings of hope and delight and a kinship with nature.

The beauty of nature seemed to have an ennobling effect upon Kunu Sangi too. In a mild tone, he spoke to Sudama, "Yes, you can compose songs, but attend to your duty without fail. If you do not, nobody will bother to give you even a grain of rice. And you also have to look after your ageing mother."

Sudama replied curtly, "I am a human being. I do not commit sins willfully."

The heavenly bodies shone over the fields as a cool and refreshing breeze gently blew. From the roads that ran by the side of the dam came bits of conversation. Dusk and twilight was the hour of Sudama, the artist. With the ukha in his hands, he crossed the fields to reach the spot where the canal broadened to turn towards the sea. At this hour, the place resounded with the songs of the birds coming home, the lapping of the seawater and the shrill cry of the cicada. In that lovely ambience of nature, the heaviness of the heart vanished. Sitting there, Sudama created music—he weaved dreams upon dreams. The music echoed in every nook and cranny of the land. It floated on the winds. The green grass looked around in search of the tune and the melody mingled itself with the approaching night.

Sudama never failed to go there in the evenings. It was there that his pent-up feelings found expression and he could forget the stress and strain of life. His boss was a good-natured man who loved to listen to his songs. Kunu informed his boss, "Sudama is our pride. It is only for a square meal that he has come so far. Routine life is not for him."

The boss looked at Sudama and smiled. It was an intimate, affable smile and Sudama felt happy. In the breaks between his work, Sudama sang. Far away stood a long line of palmyra trees. They looked so much like the workers who have come here to earn money by the sweat of their brow, thought Sudama. At dusk, wreaths of smoke rose from the oven as the field hands sat around it to cook their food. For Kunu Sangi the work was too much. "I'll go home for a few days and bring back somebody to cook my food," he announced.

Kunu Sangi came back with Basmati. Sudama did not know that Basmati would sever all ties and come. He met her one day at dusk. At first he could not believe his eyes. Then he saw it was indeed Basmati. Her shapely form was wrapped in a wet saree that could not conceal the beautiful curves of her shoulders and her breasts. Sudama's blood thickened and burned like a flame in his chest and an inexplicable passionate longing rose within him. Yes, he would build a temple for her in the unexplored region of his mind. But Kunu Sangi stood between them. Fear overpowered all emotions and passions and Sudama turned around to go. Almost immediately he stopped—the familiar call of 'Ukhababu!' bid him stop. Basmati came splashing out of the water as drops of water dripped down the curve of her breasts to her navel. She seemed to embody eternal womanhood. A look of distress spread over her face, "Why are you going away? How can you be so cruel and hard-hearted?"

Sudama pressed the ukha to his breast and said, "For me the earth is the dry land. You are the moon. No matter how much the earth desires, will the sky answer its call? Will the moon ever caress the dry earth with its lips?"

Basmati laughed a carefree laugh and dimples formed on her cheeks.

"I have come here drawn by the call of the earth."

"Is Kunu Sangi your earth then?" Sudama asked in wonder.

"I knew you would misunderstand me. It is not within the power of man to understand the sky."

From the distant huts came the sound of the tom-tom. Sudama and Basmati paused to listen. After the day's toil the field hands were dancing to the beat of the tom-tom.

It was a beautiful moonlit night. In that moonlight that flooded all corners of the earth, the leaves shimmered and the winds sang in a chorus, touching the souls of those who could hear their music. There was something different that night, and it cast a spell upon them. Basmati walked slowly towards Sudama. She came nearer and nearer until Sudama could feel the soft touch of her breasts. With a whisper Basmati said, "I would have died there." Sudama's blood flowed like fire in his veins and he drew her even closer. Basmati fell into a delicious swoon. She let him adore her and he trembled with joy. She remained still like an anchor in a rough sea as his tongue turned hunter in the twilight. It was their restoration, their recognition…

Basmati returned to her hut when the moon was high up in the sky. She thought she would be able to save herself from Kunu. But no. His eyes saw everything, noted everything. He abused Basmati, for certainly he did not bring her for the others!

One day Basmati and Sudama were returning from the fair. Basmati looked adoringly at the bangles that Sudama had bought for her. With pride he said that the bangles were signs of his love.

"Why bangles, my dear? My body bears signs of your love!" said Basmati. Then she ran away like the timid deer, her face flushing in embarrassment. Sudama ran after her only to touch her. The earth wanted to touch the sky!

But that was not destined to be. Kunu Sangi's men sprang out from the darkness with sticks in their hands and a fierce look in their eyes. Sudama could not hold Basmati's hand, neither did he get a chance to stop them. He lay there soaked red in his own blood. The ukha flew and Basmati cried out, "Don't throw it! Please don't crush it! It produces music, the music of life."

Before she could finish, Kunu Sangi appeared. He caught hold of Basmati's hand. The bangles broke one by one and the broken glass scattered all over the path. Kunu dragged Basmati telling her that he would smear her body with the signs of his love.

The silver moon was swallowed up by the dark clouds. Basmati lay by the side of the canal while Kunu Sangi took possession of her body like a vulture. The tide had come in and the sound of the rippling water could be heard from the canal. A helpless Basmati pleaded in vain to be freed, "If he is no longer alive, I must go back to his ageing mother." She sobbed aloud, "I have given her my word. She wished me to be happy."

"Will her blessings turn false?"

Kunu Sangi looked at her with fire in his eyes, "Everything is false. Only you and I, the man and the woman—we are real. We are the reality."

From a distance came the sound of the supervisor's motorcycle. It sounded like the waves of the tide.

An injured Sudama stopped him. Like an arrow-stricken bird groaning in pain, he appealed to the supervisor to save Basmati.

The supervisor turned his motorcycle towards the dam. The light from his vehicle shone on the road that was strewn with pieces of broken bangles. It did not take him long to find the way. He spotted Basmati near the edge of the canal covered in mud, her feet touching the water. Like a frightened vulture, Kunu Sangi tried to flee, stumbling across the waterlogged field. Then unable to control his balance, he splashed headlong into the water of the incoming tide.

The eternal bond of the earth and the sky washed away the sin.

Translated by Anuradha Sen

GERMAN'S MOTHER

Sons who resemble their fathers and daughters their mothers are lifelong sufferers.

German's mother believed these words to her very bones. German's father believed something else. With the veins of his throat bulging and swollen, he would say, "I don't believe your words, my wife. These are all your made-up words."

Though made-up, the axiom runs true in German's case. The poor boy looks almost like his father. Not only his appearance, but his manners, gestures, and everything else is like his father Phoring. The father looked like snake gourd, and German, a long, slender bamboo. Both the father and the son are as lean and thin as those frail toy soldiers made out of palm leaves. When they walk, their hands and legs look unsteady. German walks like a one-legged heron. Though weak, they are as steady as grasshoppers. This is why people called the father Phoring, meaning grasshopper. In these parts, the water hyacinth is called German. Floating in with the water, the leaves look oily and shiny. The densely-packed leaves draw sustenance both from the water and the soil. The plant is ever-hungry. German is a very lean and thin boy, with skin like that of an eel in colour and texture. When he laughs, his eyes sink and he looks hungry.

Really, those two eyes always look hungry. Whenever he sees food, his mouth waters.

Agrahayan is the happiest month for German and his family. Marriages, festivals, different ceremonies on different occasions take place in the village. They go to these events and come back stuffed—they don't have to cook at home. The days they get a full meal are the happiest. German's mother goes around the whole village all the time. People call her Rambhadhai. Nowadays, her job of *dhaigiri* is no longer enough to feed herself. Now people go to the hospital as soon as the labour pains begin. Coming to the end of the muddy path, she looks out vacantly. It is a really hard time for her. She has no land. This practice of child delivery is her only source of income. But it's of no use nowadays. So, even during this happy time of the year, she remains unfed. She feels nauseous as her mouth fills with the acid that her starving stomach throws up with uncomfortable and painful spasms.

As usual, she cried for Phoring Das today as well. So many years have passed. Still, she can't forget the man for a second. Dying young, the man left the family in dire distress.

German was merely a boy of twelve then. He used to graze the cows that belonged to the Pal family for ten rupees and a meal at the end of each month. That twelve-year-old German is now a young man of twenty-one years. Yet no change can be found in his physical appearance. His growth is like that of a worm-eaten tree. Rambhadhai's heart breaks and she sinks into a deep sorrow when she looks at her son's face. Then she cries some more. She sobs. Her sobs are too heart-wrenching, too anguished to bear for long. Even the cold-hearted are bound to find their eyes soaking with tears. In the early hours of the morning, Rambhadhai must cry. It is as if her heart aches if she does not cry. The food she eats remains undigested. The corners of her eyes feel raw. She cannot raise her heavy forehead either.

Of course, she has reasons to cry—her tears are not worthless. When Rambhadhai cries, the morning looks pleasant.

The sun looks tenderer than a chick that has just emerged from an egg. Obscured within the thicket of bamboo, dew drops glisten on cobwebs. It is cold everywhere. Cows walk out lazily from the cowshed. The ducks, just released from their pen, sit by the pond and shake off their drowsiness. One or two old men and the field guard walk down a desolate path. The stars are still visible in the sky. Rambhadhai chooses this hour to cry properly. Why would she not cry? She had twin sisters, Menaka and Urvashi. They got married. But then one died in childbirth, and the other followed her sister on eating the poisonous seeds of the thorny *dhatura* flower. All these bitter memories still crowd Rambhadhai's mind. The night she sees her sisters in a dream, she cries even more at dawn. Her wailing drowns the sounds of the flowing river. Is it easy to forget the dead sisters? And so, Rambhadhai goes on crying.

Not only the sisters—the horrible memory of her man brings tears to her eyes in the early hours of the morning. German was very young then. He had not even learnt to speak properly. One day he rushed to the courtyard at noon with dusty feet, and fell on the ground crying, 'O mother! Hara Ghosh has killed my father. Go and see. Father's severed body is still writhing in the pool of blood...'

Rambhadhai rushed immediately. Her hands were soaked with turmeric water as she was cooking. Phoring had brought meat from the *haat*. Before going to the field, he had told her, 'Cook it well with spices. Today we will eat a bellyful. Oh how many days it has been since we last ate meat!' But Phoring could never taste that meat. He had a bitter quarrel with the Ghosh family. It was not his fault. A minister had come from Kolkata to lease government lands. As Phoring was landless, he was given a meagre six *cotta* of land from the Ghosh family's estate. If this was his only fault, will Rambhadhai not cry?

Her cry is still heard by the members of the *panchayat*, the president of the village and everybody else. In memory of this tragic past, the gloomy mornings see Rambhadhai slapping her bare chest and cursing—'You childless people will suffer. You will die. Surely die vomiting blood. You will writhe and die. You will die of cholera. You will die with a bolt from the blue. You will never be happy. You have made me a widow. Like me, your wives and daughters will be widows. They will be barren; they will be prostitutes...' Her voice gets choked at the end in agitation. Even her saree comes undone. She sweats profusely and her bulky figure now becomes a blazing pit of fire. In anger, she shakes her head to and fro. Her fiery eyes glare at the house of Hara Ghosh.

Her cries gradually subside with the rising sun. She goes to the pond. Now she is a different woman. There is no sign of crying on her face. She looks calm. There are big, difficult tasks to perform—the day-to-day activities early in this wintry morning. The biting cold affects the village women the most as they are the ones who do the household chores in the chilly mornings. It restricts their physical movement. Yesterday in the afternoon, Rambhadhai happened to meet Kalu Sheikh in the Lakhuria market. He was going to the hospital. His thirteen-month-old son frequently wakes up from his sleep and cries incessantly. The child's belly is often distended due to indigestion. The anxious Kalu Sheikh has forgotten sleep. Every year his wife delivers a child, but they all die. The unlucky woman! Kalu Sheikh thinks that some evil has possessed his wife. Rambhadhai had gone to the market to buy kerosene and soda. There was not a drop of kerosene in her house for the last few days. The clothes have become dirty too. She needed some soda. Moreover, she had her own share of problems at home. Her son German was suffering from fever. He was bedridden for more than a month. Rambhadhai needed to buy sago to feed her son.

On her way back, she met Kalu Sheikh on the broad muddy path. It was twilight. The winter sky was covered in fog. There was absolute darkness in the Poddar family's sugarcane field.

The chattering birds perched on the babul tree were no longer clamouring. Silence prevailed everywhere. Kalu Sheikh was going up the broad muddy path. He wore a lungi. His face was sad. He carried a phial of medicine and a torch in his hand. He still had a long way to go. He was very cautious of the dangers of walking in the darkness of the night.

Rambhadhai was in a little hurry. She stopped when she heard Kalu Sheikh call her. She asked in a loud voice, 'Where did you go, Kalubhai? Is everything all right?'

Kalu Sheikh said in an anxious voice, 'I don't know what to say, German's mother. I cannot sleep for days because of the child. Every day and night, he keeps the whole neighbourhood awake. Perhaps some evil has possessed my son. He vomits everything. His belly is always swollen. So I had gone to the doctor. He has given me medicines worth seven rupees. I am now returning to my house.'

Nowadays Kalu Sheikh earns better. German's mother knows this well. Last year he built a beautiful house, with a wavy tin shed on a frame of *sal* wood. One can see the new tin shining brightly from a distance. On the very top of the house is a tin peacock. Kalu Sheikh made it himself, by cutting tin sheets. He is a professional builder of huts. People like the work of his skilful hands. So they affectionately call him Kalu Ustad.

German's mother has the eyes of a keen observer. People's sorrows and sufferings, their tricks and deceptions are all at her fingertips. Every detail about all the houses of at least ten villages is clear in her mind. After Phoring Das' death, she continued practising dhaigiri and exorcism. The nearest hospital is a long way off. Many people come to her when faced with troubles and difficulties. German is a young man only in years—but mentally he is still a child. Earlier he used to graze the cattle of the Pal family. But now he can no longer do so because of his illness. So the responsibility of the whole family falls on Rambhadhai. It is a mammoth task for her to earn even just enough for their meals.

Rambhadhai stopped suddenly. Wrapping the torn blanket around her body, she said, 'Don't worry. I'll cure your son. But you will have to spend some money. If you agree, then come to my hut tomorrow. I'll give you the blessed water. One or two gulps will cure your son.'

Kalu Sheikh comes shivering in the biting cold before dawn. It is still not light. The high bank of the muddy road is still enveloped in a dense fog that looks like floating clouds. With only a little cloth to cover her body, Rambhadhai walks the long, dewy and muddy path to Burigang. Though her eyes look sleepy, there is no sign of lethargy in her. To undergo such inhuman suffering only to earn a paltry sum of money at her age is really painful.

German is ill. He needs to be taken to a good doctor. As the trusted village doctor fails, she has to run to the town. She needs enough money to go and return, as well as for his medicines. But where will she get the money from? German's younger uncle has a business of sound systems. But that man is a hardcore miser. Rambhadhai begged him too. But he avoided her cleverly saying, "O my God! Sister-in-law, this is the off-season. There are no weddings or other such festivals. Whatever I had earned during the Durga Puja I have already spent. Now I am totally penniless." That day he had raised his hands, like the deity Gour in his well-known posture. After that, Rambhadhai did not go to anybody else for money. She has relatives in this village. But no one enquires about her in this wretched condition. It is like the relationship between spiders and their mothers.

Her suppressed cry wants to burst out as she walks on the dewy grass. She does not cry willingly. Her sorrow is deep-rooted. Her son is her only support. But he is weak both in body and mind. No knowledge, head full of cow dung—he only has uncontrollable anger in him. Who will look after him when she dies? This thought plagues Rambhadhai all the time.

She carries an iron nutcracker on a small brass pitcher. After carefully walking a small distance, Rambhadhai stops on the soaked grass of the narrow muddy path. The place is desolate and silent this early in the morning. There is a place for dead animals on the left side of the sugarcane field. In the past, Phoring Das used to go there daily. Now only Ramfal goes there. Ramfal is their kinsman. After Phoring's death, one day he touched the hands and feet of Rambhadhai and said, "O didi! Jamaidada will return no more. Don't cry and lose any more of your strength. You have to live to look after your son. You have to earn for food and clothes. So I request you to leave this wasteland to me. You are a woman. There's no need to bother about this *bhagar*. Leave it to me. Whatever I will earn from here, I promise to offer you half. I'm a true son of my father. I swear not to renege on my promise."

That was the last time Rambhadhai saw Ramfal! There is no news of his whereabouts even. He has not given her her share of the income from the bhagar for the last three years. Sometimes when they happen to meet, he hesitates and says in a rehearsed tone, "The times are very bad. Now the bhagar is totally vacant. The cattle don't die as often as they used to earlier. There are two veterinarians in the village. They inject and give medicines to the cattle when they become ill. What bad luck! I always look at the sky hungry stomach and pray repeatedly to Goddess Bhagabati. Still she remains unresponsive to my prayers. If you don't believe me, come with me and see. When you see the sprouting grass in the bhagar, you will know."

Ramfal is a liar indeed. It's his habit to lie. Today on her way to the river ghat, Rambhadhai catches him red-handed. Ramfal, who never imagined that he would run into her this early in the morning, finds himself almost as if faced with a tiger. Rambhadhai stops suddenly and looks at him like an angry animal. Ramfal is returning just after skinning a dead cow. There is blood oozing from his bundle—the whole cloth is soaked in blood. The bhagar is visible through the babul trees. Innumerable crows and vultures are hovering over the land. Rambhadhai happens to glimpse the freshly-skinned cow through the gaps between the branches of the thorny babul tree. Its huge reddish body is lying in a pool of blood.

Rambhadhai's head starts reeling at once. She cannot look at the bloody sight for long. She looks away. She shivers in fear as the oozing blood reminds her of Phoring Das. She has not been able to forget that brutal and horrible sight. It always haunts her in her sleep, in her loneliness. The horror of that sight does not vanish from her mind even after she has washed her eyes. That profound shock and distress still unsettles her. A violent wind blows over the sugarcane field. It whips up the river into waves that rise like the hood of an angry snake. Covering her chest with her saree, she glares at him angrily and thunders, "You bastard! Are you doing the right thing by letting a widow down? There is the Almighty above. He sees everything. You've not given me a single paisa in the last three years. Whenever I ask, you cry false tears. Then what is there in your bundle now? Open it. Let me see. Today I will know."

"In the morning the vultures were hovering in the sky. Seeing them, I come here at once and see a dead cow. I'm now returning after skinning it… what more can I do, didi? There are seven mouths to feed in my house. If you didn't give this bhagar to me, we, the whole family, would have starved. Could you have endured that in front of your eyes?" Having said this, Ramfal remains standing there, fear and guilt written in his eyes and face. As he is about to walk away with the bundle on the end of a stick, Rambhadhai says in a voice like thunder, "Till now I believed you were a man. Now I see you are not even a human being; you're a vulture. Where are you going with that cowhide? If there is anything human under your skin, then leave the hide to me and go. Would you betray even a woman like me?"

"What are you saying?" Ramfal gasps. "Are you doing the right thing? This is like a bolt from the blue. See, my whole family will starve and die..."

"I am not God that I will take the responsibility of your family."

Finding no other way, Ramfal fumes in anger and abuses her. Lighting a *bidi,* he says, "The bhagar was yours. That is true. But I pay the tax. Every year I have to pay a large amount of tax to the panchayat. I don't see you when it is time to pay tax. But you shout to get your share. This bhagar is now mine. You have no right over it."

"You son of a shit-eater! Shut up! Wait, I'll show you...!" Putting down the small brass pitcher, Rambhadhai rushes to beat him. Seeing no way out, Ramfal picks up the bundle and runs away like a frightened fox. He slips once on the slippery grass, but rises again. He looks behind like a throttled heron and gasps like a strangled goat. Rambhadhai cannot control her desperation and rage and covering her face, she bursts into tears. The fresh morning breeze turns stifling at once. She feels even more helpless and alone in the desolate field. Eventually, she wipes her tears and slowly moves towards Burigang.

In this chilly morning, it is not easy to take a plunge in the river and fill the pitcher. After filling the small pitcher, Rambhadhai moves towards the sandy shore of the river, shivering in the cold. The sun rises, its gentle rays falling on the sands. The wind near the river is always wild. The *kadakhnocha* birds on both sides of the Burigang have already woken up on this shiny morning. The lean-bodied birds look very bright today.

The meat of these birds is tastier than dove meat. Phoring Das used to catch birds in the jungles. German was his faithful companion. He was very attached to his father. Rambhadhai ruminates that perhaps her man spent the whole day by the side of this river when he used to come to the bhagar. Once when German was in her womb, she wished to eat the meat of these kadakhnocha birds. Phoring got ready to go at once, almost forgetting to bathe and eat for many of the following days. At last he returned one evening with some birds in his hands, and jokingly said, "Here, take the birds that you craved for so long. Eat to your satisfaction so that my son who will soon come into this world would not slaver for them..."

And today that man is lost somewhere like the birds. Thinking of him, her eyes fill with tears like the wet river bank. It was too early for him to die. It is Hara Ghosh who killed him. He was alone against those ten men armed with sticks. Yet Phoring resisted in protest. But he could not survive the terrible blow of the axe. Rambhadhai went to the police station and filed a case against Hara Ghosh. The police even came and arrested Hara Ghosh with proper evidence. They promised that proper justice would be served. Possibly, Hara Ghosh might be hanged. But Hara Ghosh was imprisoned for not even a year. Much before his term was completed, he returned from jail. Later it was heard that the whole case was dismissed only because of money. Hara Ghosh was found not guilty, and he was released.

German has become hot-headed since then. If he happens to hear the name of Hara Ghosh, he seethes in anger. He shouts and says, "Mother, I will not let him go. I must take revenge." Unfortunately, there is not much strength in his body, but his anger is that of a Royal Bengal Tiger. As the days go by, he is gradually becoming thinner and thinner in front of her eyes. His ribs have become visible. Being a mother, how can she endure this! That's why Rambhadhai goes out in the chilly winter mornings—only to get some money.

German did not follow his father's profession. He never even visited the bhagar. Knives and razors for skinning dead animals are the most detestable things to him. Sometimes when his mother rebukes him, he remains silent with a gloomy face. Then in anger, he snaps his hair, curses his lot and says, "God has blessed me with life in this world, but alas! I cannot hold anything properly in these thin, weak hands. But you see mother, I will not surrender. I must take revenge."

Bitter and enraged from his very childhood, German has grown into an angry young man. He cannot forget even for a day the cruel image of the murderer Hara Ghosh. He always waits for an opportunity to take revenge. His eyes dazzle in a primitive anger even in darkness.

After taking the blessed water from Rambhadhai, Kalu Sheikh returned to his house. Taking her dues from him, Rambhadhai is about to enter her hut when she is called by Naran Morol. He is a tall and petulant man with a muffler around his neck. With his hands on his cheeks, in a mournful tone he calls Rambhadhai, "O Masi! I'll surely die of toothache. Yesterday, I could not sleep the whole night. I brushed my teeth ten times with tobacco. I even tried some other means. But no relief at all. So, I rushed to you. Please remove the caries from my teeth. I will pay you handsomely."

Rambhadhai turns her back after hearing Naran Morol's words. She has a good reputation in this locality for cleaning dental caries. But she is not paid enough. People find it difficult to pay even one rupee and twenty-five paise. Sometimes, this makes Rambhadhai angry. Whatever she earns for her livelihood is only from these practices. If she is not paid even this meagre amount, it becomes really difficult for her. Yet, Rambhadhai endures everything as she has to live among them.

This is the tradition in the village. She cannot change it in a single day. German says, "Why don't you say anything? You work as a midwife. Your hands become soaked in the blood from their wombs. But you get only this meagre amount after a year. How can people do this? Will you remain unfed throughout the year? Why can't the people feel your suffering?"

German says nothing wrong. It is Rambhadhai's duty to assist in the delivery of the village women. She is summoned even before the labour pain begins. Nobody pays her money at the end. She returns almost empty-handed. They say, "German's mother, we won't be able to pay you anything now but we will send ten bundles of paddy to your house at harvest time. Now just have some of this sweet."

Rambhadhai says defiantly, "Tasting sweets is not enough. This time you've been blessed with a son. Give me a brassy salver. If you don't, who will? I solely depend on you."

By the time she has cleaned the caries of Naran Morol, she is very late. The sun has already begun to pour heat. Two goats still tied in the shed are bleating bitterly. It seems that if they are somehow released, they will jump on Hara Ghosh's crops. Only the other day, the big goat was released from the cowshed of Hara Ghosh. German beat it so much that it almost died. Rambhadhai rushed from the hut and pacified him. German burst in anger and said, "Why does it go there? I'll break its legs! I beat it so frequently, yet it does not learn its lesson!"

"That's why this poor creature is called goat!" Rambhadhai smiles on seeing her son's anger against the animal. It makes German even more furious. He goes into the mud hut with a sullen face.

Rambhadhai remains so busy in household chores that she hardly has time to breathe. Today she has to visit two houses to massage the new mothers. She eagerly expects to get at least one kilo rice; it will help in these bad days. But the thought of German's fragile health brings tears to her eyes. She hears footsteps of imminent doom and shrinks back in fear as she observes him from a distance. German looks so thin that she can't recognise her own son. The eyes have sunken into their sockets. Helpless, Rambhadhai's tears roll down her face and collect at her chin.

She stands in front of German with the boiled sago, examines his temperature and says, "I see the temperature has decreased a little today."

German says nothing and lowers his head to the ground. Winter or summer or rain, everything is the same in this house of straw. Pulling the blanket, he takes the glass of sago.

A sudden flicker of hope lights up the eyes of Rambhadhai. She consoles him, "Take it, my child. I'll give you some rice with *shingi* fish soup." She says, "Even big *rajbhog* sweets taste bitter when you are ill."

This time German coughs badly. Pressing his breast with his hands, he looks at his mother with painful and helpless eyes. Wiping his face on his sleeve, he says in a feeble voice, "This is an incurable disease. I know that I have been attacked by the fatal TB. My uncle suffered from it. Is it possible that I will not be affected by it?"

"Oh, how can you say this?" Rambhadhai's lips quiver in fear. She somehow controls herself and says, "Never say these unlucky words. Does nobody suffer from fever? Your father used to fall ill twice or thrice every year. Yet he did not lose his courage."

"But my fever is different from my father's. My fever has attacked my mind too. Oh mother, don't think about it. When my anguished mind is pacified, the fever will be cured by itself."

German looks at the narrow path to the maize field in the distance. In his childhood, they used to find oysters on this narrow path, and used to rub them against the cement floor of the school building to make knives to peel mangoes with. His companions used to say, "You are so addicted to knives. Your scythe is so sharp. You make it look shiny just by a little rubbing against the stony slab. You can cut a big banyan tree in a single stroke."

German would become more agitated after hearing their words. His lean body blazed in anger. The severed head of his father tormented his mind. There was no sign of weakness in his eyes then—they glowed like fireflies. Sweat rolled down his hair, ears, neck and chest to his heels. He gasped like a cow. With fiery eyes he glared at Hara Ghosh's brick house. Pulling at his hair in uncontrollable wrath, he hollered, "*Sala*, you killed my father! I'll not leave you. Just let me grow up. Then I will chop off your head!"

German gradually grows up to become a thin and lean-bodied man who looks like the younger sibling of a sal tree. A deep anger is rooted in his mind. Rambhadhai is often scared to look at him. There is not much flesh on his bones, yet his anger is unparalleled.

There is utmost poverty in their house. Nowadays Rambhadhai does not make much from her dhaigiri. She manages somehow with whatever she makes from her other practices—giving people blessed water or oil and uttering incantations to cure different ailments. Both the mother and the son eat a handful of rice during the day and only some boiled flour at night. Although German is thin, he eats like a grown man. He is a growing boy. Even a whole salver of rice is not enough for him. Seeing him eat so much rice, the neighbours used to joke, "Your son eats like a big cow. He has so ravenous a belly that it will digest everything." Rambhadhai has no funds now. How can she keep her son well-fed? That year people found themselves in dire straits as the flood had wreaked havoc. For her, it's a matter of shame to ask people for money. Is it right to beg when there is still strength left in the body to work? Rambhadhai's heart always wails when she thinks about German. She gazes at her son and feels bewildered.

It was the month of Ashwin. The paddy fields were filled with *kash* flowers. The brimming river glistened in the sun. The lands were lush with crops. So people were in a happy mood. The whole household of the Pal family were jubilant at the marriage ceremony of Palbabu's elder son. Someone was needed to clean the leftovers of the marriage feast. Rambhadhai came to know of it. She went to Palbabu and said, "Oh babu, let me clean the leftovers. The times are very bad for me. My son insists on eating meat. Kindly allow me to put together a meal from the leftovers, only to give some meat to my poor child. He has always been very thin from the time of his birth. I hope that the meat from the marriage feast will do well for his poor health."

Rambhadhai's appeal somehow touched Palbabu. He agreed at once. He thought that getting someone to clean the leftovers free of cost was a matter of luck. Rambhadhai brought a pail filled with chicken and fish bones, spicy mixed vegetables and other leftovers. When she was returning home early in the morning, she looked jubilant. Seeing the leftover food of the babus, her joy knew no bounds. Her son had not tasted meat for such a long time. Today he would get to eat a bellyful. A cupful of chicken could be gathered from a full pail of the leftovers. And six puffy *luchis* soaked in chickpea *dal*.

When he saw the leftovers, German was furious. He was speechless with anger for some time. At last he calmed down and said, "You take it, mother, if you are so hungry! You've collected the leftovers from the babu's house throughout the night! Don't you have any dignity? Are you not their nurse-midwife? What will be the condition of that child who comes out from the womb treated by the touch of your dirty hands? He may devour the whole world. Chhi! Chhi! Why do you always forget that you too have some dignity as a human being?"

"We, the poor, should not have this gentleman-like attitude. Your father too could not earn anything and used to depend on his wife. But still he always spoke like a *nawab*."

"My father was a venomous hooded snake, not a worm. I am his son! Do you think that I'll eat the leftovers of Hara Ghosh? It'll never happen in my life. That Hara Ghosh too went to the marriage feast of the Pal family. If I am such a huge burden to you, then bring me some poison. I will ingest it and die. Then you'll be free to live, cleaning the blood from the genitals of these men's wives, and eating their leftovers."

There was enough poison in her son's words to burn her being. Rambhadhai's whole body felt scalded by that poison. She felt dizzy. Walking unsteadily, she vomited up the luchis and the spiced meat behind the haystack.

From then on, she never goes to collect leftovers. If someone calls her, she refuses at once. German is very happy about this and says, "God has blessed us with these two hands and two legs. We'll work hard to live—there is no regret in that. But there is no dignity in filling our stomachs with the leftovers of others. If you need money, just go to the field and collect some *kolmi* leaves. Sell those in the market. There is enough dignity in that. Nobody has to suffer any humiliation at all."

Rambhadhai now collects kolmi leaves and goes to the village market with a full basket. Putting them on an old saree, she sells them. However, she does not do this during the harvest season—she has to do a lot of things then. This is the time when she collects her dues for the whole year. Those who cannot pay money give small bundles of paddy. In such cases, she has to bargain a lot. Sometimes the number of bundles increases from ten to fifteen. Rambhadhai carries these paddy bundles back home on her head.

Rambhadhai went to the field after giving a massage to two new mothers in different houses. Her neck aches now under the weight of the small paddy bundles. Her whole body is dusty and covered with bits of straw. German remains in bed all day. He cannot rise. The days on which he feels good, he goes out to the village temple. The sky is cloudy today. It remains foggy for a long time in the morning. It's cold too. After a bath in the pond, as Rambhadhai is about to ignite the clay stove to begin cooking, she hears German uttering a painful cry from inside their small bamboo-walled mud house. Without lighting the stove, she rushes into the house in fear and asks, "What has happened to you, my son? Why do you look like this?"

His whole body is sweating profusely. The dirty shirt he is wearing is soaked in sweat. The torn blanket is lying at his feet. Seeing her, he somehow rises. He gasps and says, "Oh mother! I saw my father in a dream. He just stood near my head. There were no tears in his eyes. Only blood. He shook me and said, 'Oh son! This fever will not leave you. My heat has worked on you. Hara Ghosh killed me unjustly. And the people of the whole village witnessed it without any protest. No one asked for justice. My heart is still seething with rage. So I have come back again. I have nowhere to go. I left you and your mother to suffer. You are my son. Take revenge if you can. Then I will come no more to vex you.' Now tell me Ma, can my fever go away after this?"

Covering her face, Rambhadhai sobs, "Oh beta, be quiet. The man often appears in my dreams too. My whole body freezes in fear then. I cannot look at his red eyes. He urges me to take revenge too. But I cannot make him understand how difficult it is."

"If you can't take revenge, I must." Saying this, he takes out the sharpened scythe from underneath his bed. He holds it tight and says, "Look, it is sharper than an axe!"

Rambhadhai is shocked and afraid. She says, "Oh my son, dear son, put it back. I've already lost one. I don't want to lose you, my only remaining hope."

They stand and look at each other with frightened eyes in that dreadfully still house. The cold air blowing in makes them feel even colder and weaker. German says, "If the squirrel can build a bridge, then will I not be able to perform such an easy task? Your mind is weak, so you think of the worst."

In the afternoon, the air is still. The clouds loom like a huge monster. A vulture is tossed from the tamarind tree by the storm. The crows are cawing. German falls unconscious in bed. The village doctor says, "The symptoms are not good. Take your son to the town. He needs a blood test."

On hearing the doctor's words, Rambhadhai loses her mind. She cries for an hour and curses her lot. She even abuses Hara Ghosh in a loud voice.

By evening German has regained his senses. Rising from the bed, he pours some water from the pitcher and gulps it down. Then he goes back to his bed. He can't sleep. The bugs bite him. The mosquitoes buzz near him. In insufferable pain, German folds his legs and lies like a dead man. The straw house is filled with cold air. Outside the birds are on the way to their nests, chirping. German longs to have his mother beside him. The pain makes him more depressed. In a faint voice, he cries out, "Mother! Mother!" He turns on his side. Suddenly, he is startled by the sound of thunder. The water of the Burigang rises. The dewy leaves shiver. The goats tied on the terrace bleat hoarsely. The whole atmosphere becomes darker. Cuckoo feathers float in the air. Bolts of lightning flash across the sky. A chilly wind is blowing. He trembles and the chill spreads from his chest to his veins.

German rises from the bed again. This time he has wrapped his body with not just the cloth but also an old rag. Yet he feels even colder. He shivers violently. He cannot see anything in the darkness; he can't even feel his own existence. Somehow he lights the lantern. There is no hope of Rambhadhai coming back. She has gone to the Bene's house to mortgage their utensils. She has no other way. These brass utensils are nothing to her when her son's life is in danger. She has taken everything from the house that she has earned so far from her dhaigiri. She did not pay any heed to German's appeals.

Sitting in a corner near the muddy wall, a cat is crying ominously. To German it sounds like his mother's cries. There is no strength left in him to get up and drive the cat away.

It starts raining harder as the night grows darker. A cold wind sweeps through the silent village. Piercing the thatched roof, the rain falls on the bed and soaks the torn rags that German is wrapped in. He shivers uncontrollably.

After two hours of heavy rain, the whole yard is waterlogged. Still the clouds look ominous. The raindrops pierce like sharp arrows of glass. German's mother enters the house, soaked and shivering with cold. The ten-rupee notes folded in her hands are crumpled and soggy. Yet, she grips them tightly. Tomorrow she will take her son to the town by the morning bus. The poor boy needs good treatment. The village doctor has failed to diagnose the fever.

German says, "This fever will not leave me, Ma. The fever is in my mind. The night I see father in my dreams, the fever is worse. And I can't open my eyes. I feel a lot of pain, Ma."

"Be quiet." She changes her saree and dries the notes slowly in the heat of the lantern. German says, "I'll not go to the town. If I go, I will die."

Rambhadhai bursts into tears on hearing her son's words. Lightning flashes in the sky to the south-west. The babul and the banana trees sway in the mad wind. Big raindrops fill the yard. Rambhadhai closes the door. She places a damp cloth on her son's forehead and sits still beside him.

The night grows, yet the rain does not stop. Rambhadhai repeatedly changes the damp cloth on German's forehead. He lies motionless and her eyes are moist—with tears or with raindrops, it is hard to say. German says, his lips quivering, "Oh mother, bring another *kantha* and put it on my body. I am very cold."

When Rambhadhai brings her own kantha and goes to put it on German's body, someone outside calls in an aggrieved voice, "German's mother?"

Rambhadhai could clearly hear someone calling her. She opens the latch and says, "It is Hara Ghosh!"

Holding an umbrella over his head and shivering, Hara Ghosh stood there in the cold rain.

"What do you want?" Rambhadhai screams in anger. "Why are you here? What do you need here?"

Hara Ghosh's voice is on the verge of breaking. He mumbles, "My pregnant wife writhes in labour pain. You have to come to my house once. There is no way we can take her to the hospital five miles away on this stormy night. Even Malatidhai is not in her house tonight. She has gone to her daughter's house." Suddenly he stops, takes a deep breath and looks at her with the eyes of a criminal.

German's mother looks at him, seething. She looks closely at the man standing in front of her. Her face and eyes harden. Her voice trembling with cruel rage, she says, "You are the man responsible for my wretched condition. Yet how dare you step inside my yard and appear before me? Don't your legs tremble? Doesn't your heart break?"

Hara Ghosh remains silent. Even the rain, the winds and the water do not seem to forgive him. He shivers like the leaves of a tamarind tree. After a long wait of ten years, he is going to be the father of a child. People call him the unlucky childless man. They think it is a sin to look at his face before an auspicious work. Will that bad reputation finally come to an end? The poor woman has been writhing in labour pain like a sacrificed goat. There are no other women in the house. The whole floor is flooded with blood. "Go, call German's mother" is all she could say before she fainted. Hara Ghosh rushed to the house of Malatidhai in the heavy storm and rain. Failing to find the midwife there, he immediately rushed to the house of Phoring Das. To him it seemed more painful than walking barefoot on hot iron.

German's mother says, "Get out! I don't want to see your face. These are your very hands that wiped the vermilion from my forehead, broke the bangles on my wrists and made me forlorn—even more helpless than a beggar."

"Oh, German's mother! To err is human. Is there no forgiveness for my sin? No punishment?" Hara Ghosh stood there with his head lowered. "You have a scythe at home? Here, I lower my head. Behead me. I'll lie here in two pieces. Yet, promise me that you'll go to my house just once. If the woman dies in childbirth, both the tree and the fruit will be lost. Both lives will be lost! It is better that I die instead."

Hearing Hara Ghosh's words, German comes out ferociously with the shining scythe in his hand. His face and eyes are red with fever and rage. His legs tremble. Yet he stands face to face before Hara Ghosh and roars, "What my father could not, I will do. Come, you son of a pig! Today I will cut you into pieces."

Raising the scythe over his head, German is ready to strike. Hara Ghosh remains standing there with his head bowed and says, "Why are you waiting? Kill me. If I can die by your hands, the burden of my sin will diminish a little. Strike me. Here, I lay my head before you."

Rambhadhai snatches the scythe from a desperate German and forces him to return to bed, saying, "The man has come to my house and surrendered. Will you kill him? Chhi! Don't you have any conscience? Even in my dreams I never thought that my own son could be so ungrateful!"

Rambhadhai grabs Hara Ghosh by the neck and drives him out of her courtyard. The man goes back in anguish and shame. His parting words touch her deeply. He said, "If she was your own daughter, could you sit idle here? All of this is because of my wicked deeds. I will not come again to show you this wicked face. Let the worst happen. If she dies, tomorrow I'll take her for cremation to the burning *ghat*."

After Hara Ghosh's departure, Rambhadhai loses her mind. Dhaigiri is a profession where one must go whenever one is called. Otherwise this skill handed down from generation to generation will no longer be needed. Besides, if people do not respond when their fellow beings are in danger, they are no better than animals. Will she lower herself to that position? In utter confusion and turmoil, she presses her forehead into her palms. Then, she submits to her own conscience. She picks up the bundle of dry clothes. As she is about to go out, German calls her from behind, "Where are you going, mother, in such rough weather?"

"To Hara Ghosh's house." Without saying another word, Rambhadhai quickly goes out and begins walking along the muddy path. The sounds of crickets and other insects emanate from the bushes on both sides of the muddy road. On this cold winter night, even the frogs croak loudly to produce a little warmth. Yet, German's mother feels as if her throat is about to choke as some unknown thoughts plague her mind. Her steps gradually slow down although she tries harder to walk quickly. She presses the bundle close to her breast. She starts panting as she walks. She has not walked this path for so many years. But she has no fear at all. Rather, she is desperate to reach. The fainted woman must be rescued. A child must be taken out from the darkness of the womb.

One who can do this is never an ordinary being. Maybe she has no food in her belly, no decent clothes on her body—yet she is the nurse-midwife. The newborn child cannot see the mother just after birth. The nurse is its first mother. Cleaning the blood and pus of ten months and ten days with her own hands, she shows the child the first light of this world. Can a child forget her?

A dim lantern burns. Hara Ghosh sits before it, his head lowered like an insect. He has called the poor woman many times, but there has been no response. He has pulled at his hair looking at her fixed and senseless face.

Seeing German's mother enter the courtyard, he regains strength in his body. He covers his face and begins to cry in remorse.

German's mother warns him, saying, "Is this the time to cry? Go bring me a big tumbler of lukewarm water as quickly as possible. Get me some old, dry clothes, if you have any. And make a fire from the cow dung. Can anybody live without warmth in such biting cold?"

Rambhadhai then enters the house. She faces great difficulty in taking the child out from the womb—all of her past experience seeming almost to give way. But she wins at last. As soon as the baby comes out, it cries loudly. The mother opens her eyes.

When she returns home, Rambhadhai sees German leaning on the stone slab and sharpening the big knife. Hearing her footsteps, he looks up at her and says accusingly, "Are you back after tasting sweets in Hara Ghosh's house? Good! Very good! The snake that once bit you, you have now returned after kissing it! Are you a human being or God?"

Rambhadhai says in an unperturbed voice, "I am German's mother."

"Then why didn't you avenge my father's killing? Is it the water of the Burigang that flows in your veins instead of blood? Oh mother! All this time I thought of you as God. Today I see you are just a lump of soil. One who has no rage, no contempt. Nothing. What can she be but a mere lump of soil?"

"She is only a mother. What kind of mother she is nobody else can understand—only a mother can."

"Enough of all these riddles. Tell me, what did Hara Ghosh give you?"

"He wanted to give me the deed of the leased land. But I did not take it."

"Did you leave without taking anything from him, the one who rubbed salt in your open wound? If I were in your place, I would have strangled the newborn baby. Many die in the labour room. Nobody would have come to know."

"I too tried. I tried. But I could not do it, my son. The baby's eyes looked so much like your father's. My hands grew inert as I was going to strangle it. The baby began to cry bitterly. Its fingers were as soft as boiled spinach. It had no strength at all." Having said this, German's mother plunges into silence. She looks out at the field for a time with wide eyes. At last she rubs her eyes and says in a grief-stricken voice, "Lord Sri Krishna was born in the prison of Kansa. Later the same Krishna killed Kansa. Don't worry, my son. Events of the Dwaparyug still happen in this Kaliyug."

After a long pause, German says, "Oh mother, I no longer have a fever."

Translated by Arun Pramanik

HUNGER

Badla heard about it from Dasu. He was drinking tea at Dasu's tea stall and so was Putli. Putli forgot everything when she had something to eat or drink, so great was her desire for food. Naturally, she was unaware of Dasu who stared with lecherous eyes at the fine curves of her exposed breasts. He kept on staring hungrily. Only when he saw that the others had been observing him, he turned his eyes away and ordered them to leave his shop.

Like the other days, Badla had set out early in the morning to wander about in the village. Putli went along with him. Badla couldn't say no to her. The two of them had not tasted rice in two days. Their skins were rough and dirty. Putli said, "Whatever we get we will divide equally. Agreed?"

Badla did agree. He had no other way out. He knew too well how difficult begging would be. The village was ravaged by the cyclone. Huts were broken, crops were damaged. The loss had made everyone peevish and ill-tempered. So, it was useless going from door to door. Nobody had any sympathy for beggars at this time. They were busy repairing the damages. It was on Badla and those like him that they vented their anger. Some even came out with sticks to chase the beggars away.

Having finished his tea, Badla asked Dasu for water. He would wash his cup and keep it. Every day Dasu gave him tea in that stained and cracked cup. There was no separate cup for Putli. She could drink tea in any cup. Perhaps because she was a girl, and a well-built one for that matter.

Badla lit a *bidi* and waited for Putli to join him. Dasu poured some water into the kettle, set it on the oven and said, "Badlakhuro, tomorrow is Haro Ghosh's *shraddha* ceremony. A lot of preparations are going on. The whole village will attend."

To Badla who was insatiably hungry, shraddha meant only one thing: eating good food. He knew it. He became restless and started swinging his legs continuously.

The day before the shraddha, rice would be taken and kept under the shade of the *jeol* trees. Haro Ghosh's trees were on the northern side of the fen. Ghosh's son would take all the choicest dishes that his father liked to eat. This thought made Badla distracted. Dasu said to him, "What's wrong? Why do you look so pale?"

"Nothing." Badla stood up. His thoughts merged with the confused uproar from Haro Ghosh's house where preparations for the last rites were going on in full swing.

Haro Ghosh had been a kind and sympathetic man. His son Panchu, the head of the village, would surely allow the poor and the destitute to eat. Putli came and stood before him. She was rather impatient.

"Come on. What are you waiting for?"

"Where will we go?"

"I don't want to go to Ganeshbabu's house. He is too rude. He raises his stick to strike for no reason."

"Eh! It's not that easy. If he strikes, strike back." Badla smiled. He looked longingly at Putli but did not voice his opinion. Just a few days back, Ganeshbabu had chased him out. "Get out!" he had snarled. "Are you not ashamed? You come every day to eat.

You shameless creature! If I see you here again tomorrow, I'll break your bones!"

Badla did not know what to say. His mouth watered for the *khichudi* that is distributed at such places for free. But such was his luck. Many had told him to work. Surely that is better than begging, they had argued. Badla always remained quiet. Why should he work? For whom should he work? He was alone in this world. His wife had died five years back. His ancestral house was mortgaged. He had neither the means nor the ways to get it back. He came back to his village after having wandered about here and there for nearly one and a half years. He looked more and more like a vagabond with his long hair and beard. The wrinkles on his face drooped close to his moustache every time he spoke or smiled making him look all the more ugly. Mucus leaked from his eyes while foam formed at the corners of his mouth if he spoke continuously. People couldn't speak to him. They didn't want to. Every time he opened his mouth to speak, a foul smell made the listener want to vomit. To add to it, he spit saliva all over the place. That was not all. Badla's waist twisted in a funny manner when he walked. He used to work as a helper for a professional hut-builder. He had fallen down while working on the rooftop once and hurt himself badly. The injury in his waist was still not cured. His heels were cracked and he wore slippers made of tyre rubber. They were strapped to his feet with rope so that when he ran, he did not leave his slippers behind. He had developed the habit of wearing slippers while in town.

Putli called out to him again reminding him of the rising heat. Badla picked up his side bag and started limping along. Dasu was busy with his customers. Many of them were waiting eagerly for the newspaper. Putli said in feigned anger, "Is it possible for us to wait and take rest in one place for such a long time? It is so hot, but we have to make a living by begging. It will be very difficult. I feel so tired and thirsty."

The sun and the rain came down with equal force on this village. When the storm blew, everything seemed to be topsy-turvy. During floods, men and cattle suffered together. It was difficult to spot even a patch of dry land. What fascination Putli had for such a village she alone knew. Although she had no shelter in this village, yet it seemed to be her very own.

After a long time, Badla lit a bidi. Almost at once Putli said, "Give me one."

"You?"

"Yes, why not?"

Putli's words and manners were direct like those of the *babughar*. Sharp and direct. Badla liked listening to her. Very often Putli would tell him of her background. She came from a family of workers who were quite well-to-do. But as luck would have it, her husband died too soon. He was caught red-handed one day when he was busy taking coal from the engine. Her mother-in-law had chased her out saying her presence spelt ill luck for the family. Since then Putli had been working and begging. Finally she had reached the village. Her sensual and fleshly body was responsible for her difficulties. Whoever saw her wanted her and offered her money for a moment's pleasure. Previously she slept at the place where public functions were held. The other day the potato-seller had woken her up at midnight. When Putli understood what the matter was, she abused him and bit him. The man had then run away.

Badla was scared to touch Putli—her anger made him stop every time he wanted to. She understood everything in no time and abused and cursed all who made dirty advances. Putli had nothing to eat and no place to stay, but she was conscious of her self-respect and guarded it fiercely. How cutting her remarks were!

Scratching her head, Putli pulled out a louse. She said, "How hot it is today!"

"Come, let us take the path through the mango grove. We can go without any trouble then. There's plenty of shade," Badla said. Putli liked the suggestion. They crossed the main road and turned towards the grove. It was quite a big one, about four acres in all. The path across it was covered with dry yellow leaves that produced a sharp, crackling noise when walked upon.

"Beautiful shade, isn't it?" Putli's face flooded with joy.

"Yes," said Badla. He was very hungry. He had had no rice for the past two days. Only some dry bread that Dasu had given him that was too little to satisfy his overpowering hunger. Thank God there was enough water to fill his belly with.

"I remember my husband when I walk down shaded paths like this. After every storm, he used to go out with a sack to collect mangoes."

"What did you do with the mangoes?"

"Why, pickle, sour broth, dried mango, mango jam. He liked all these very much—especially the dried pieces of green mango preserved in salt."

Badla could not control himself. He swallowed hard and said, "It's been a long time since I tasted fish in a sour broth. Can you cook it one day?"

"No food, no shelter—how will I cook?" Putli turned around and smiled, "This is not the season for mangoes. Let the time come, I will cook it for you."

Badla was lost in thought. His mind travelled down the long-lost path to those days when his wife Lakshmi used to cook his favourite dish, pumpkin curry with spices. The taste still lingered in his mouth. At the mention of Lakshmi, Putli's eyes widened with envy. Moving the dry leaves carelessly with her feet, she said, "Will I be able to cook like Lakshmi? My husband did not like what I cooked for him."

"Did your husband work in an office?"

"Of course he did. Every morning he used to go out brushing his teeth to the station. He had a pact with the engine driver.

The moment he raised the long pole that had currency notes attached to it, the driver dropped a basket full of coal. Then he used to sell the coal. Sometimes he took me to film shows. Do you know, I have watched Dara Singh's films."

"Dara Singh? Who is he?"

"O ma, this man doesn't know anything!" She covered her face with the end of her saree and her eyes suddenly filled with tears. She said, "My husband was as strong and well-built as Dara Singh. Yet we had no children. We went from temple to temple. We promised to offer a sacrifice to God if our prayers were answered. But nothing came of it." Putli sighed and tried to wipe her tears.

"You are crying?"

Putli wiped her eyes carefully and said, "No, why will I cry? I have no one to cry for."

Standing under the shade of the mango tree, Putli looked sad and forlorn. Seeing her, Badla's heart was filled with sorrow. Putli looked like a statue. With her folded hands pressed upon her chest, she was still crying silently.

Badla took her hand. Putli did not stop him. She raised her eyes to look at him once. That was enough. Badla was filled with a desire to possess her. "You touched me, is it?" she asked, her lips trembling. Badla held her hand even more firmly. He said in a low voice, "I am also unlucky. Lakshmi was pregnant thrice but every time it ended in a miscarriage." Putli's eyes grew misty on hearing this. She did not know how she stood straight. Balancing herself on her toes, she held Badla's hand tightly. Then she lay down, dishevelled, on the dry yellow leaves. Badla became impatient. High up on the trees birds fluttered their wings. There was silence everywhere. Badla looked around once and then thrust his bearded face into Putli's heavy breasts. Putli cried out in pain. Pushing Badla's thin body away, she growled at him, "You good-for-nothing! Can't give me anything to eat but always on the lookout for quick lovemaking."

"Keep quiet." He could not stop himself. He was too enamoured with her body. The fullness of her body fanned the flames of desire in him and drew him towards her like a magnet.

Putli would not keep quiet. She kept on talking as their bodies merged. After some time, Putli draped her saree and fixed it properly back in place. Looking at Badla she said softly, "I have not eaten anything in two days. No one likes all this while hungry." Badla clenched his jaw and said, "I will give you rice. Come to me."

Putli did not. She started walking backwards till she reached the end of the mango grove. She looked over the dense, wild growth and her eyes met the crystal-clear water of the pond and the cement landing steps leading to it. Right in the middle of the pond, like a nose ring the *shapla* flowers adorned the water.

Putli went down the steps. She splashed water on her face and then started swimming with force. She swam around in circles in the water happily. Badla shouted out, "Come out! Putli, come out! You will fall sick. Who will look after you then?" Putli pulled out some stalks of the water-lily along with the roots. She came out draped in the wet saree that left her arms, neck and a part of her heavy breasts bare. She looked at her hands and then divided the lilies equally. Holding out half of the lilies, she said to Badla, "Here, eat these. It will calm your appetite." Then she twisted her long hair into a knot and put a single lily on the left side of the bun, and said, laughing, "See, I have dressed up like a queen." Badla could not take his eyes off her. Putli laughed aloud. She said, "You are sick. All right, come to the school ground after dusk with some rice. Let me see your ability."

Putli walked away, her hips swaying. Badla started dozing. By and by, exhaustion overtook him. His nerves soothed and muscles relaxed as he fell fast asleep and saliva dribbled down the corner of his mouth. Late in the evening, the bites of the large black ants woke him up. He sat up with a jerk. Putli was nowhere around. It was dark. He stood up hurriedly, wiping the drool off his face. A cup of tea would have helped. He remembered it was the day on which solemn obsequies were to be performed in memory of Haro Ghosh. Rice and other delicacies would be taken to the fen in the evening.

Badla started running as fast as his legs could carry him. Then he stopped. His legs gave away. But Dasu's words came back to his mind and he started walking towards Ghosh's house. The dog barked twice. In fear, his waist started paining again after many days.

Putli had often told him it was nothing serious, only rheumatic pain. A slight massage with the balm that has been preserved for twelve years would help him. From where would Badla get it? He peeped through the door of the backyard. Sweetmeats were being prepared. Haro Ghosh's grandson saw him, and wrinkling his nose in disgust he called out to his mother, "See, mother, Mad Badla has come. Oh, what a foul smell!"

Cowering away in hesitation, Badla tried to smell his garments and his bag. He found nothing wrong. His dirty shirt caught his attention; it annoyed him even though it was his favourite shirt.

Haro Ghosh's eldest grandson came towards him and pushed him cruelly. Badla fell down and then turned around to look at him with eyes full of tears. Seeing him in that condition, the children started laughing. Badla managed to get up somehow and he started running. Suddenly a broken piece of brick came and hit him in the waist from behind.

This sudden attack proved too much. Badla fell down in a heap of cow dung. After half an hour, when he came back to his senses, he saw with wonder Panchu Ghosh going towards the fen. In one hand he held a big basket and in the other a lantern. Behind him was a young boy of about twelve years. Badla stood up. Keeping a safe distance, he began walking. He felt scared when he reached the *arjun* tree. He felt terribly cold. The empty field seemed to echo his thoughts. The last time he had come, it was a narrow save. Paltu's pet dog had seen him and had run after him to tear him to bits. Badla had to jump into the water to save himself.

There was risk involved. He hid himself behind the trees. Haro Ghosh's son passed him holding the cane basket. Behind him went his younger son, with a betelnut on a betel leaf, a new towel and a new cushion. Haro Ghosh always went to inspect the fields with a new towel thrown over his shoulder and an umbrella. So his son would keep a new towel and an umbrella for him there.

Badla left the arjun tree behind and crossed the fields. It was no longer dark. The pump was drawing in water. After some time, the place would be lit up with electric lights. So Badla had to change his route. He went by the sugarcane field. Panchu Ghosh would not take this roundabout way.

Badla came and stood near the fen. There was no moon, only stars that twinkled by their own light. The smell of stale grass filled the entire area.

Haro Ghosh's son was near the water. He washed his hands and came up. He broke the earthen pot as was the custom. Then he placed a banana leaf on which he started keeping the food items that he had brought.

"Won't you offer some salt to Dadu?" asked the young boy. "Won't you give him water?"

Panchu had forgotten the water. He filled an earthen bowl with water. Then he kneeled and began speaking aloud to his dead father. The young fellow began asking questions again.

"You didn't give the umbrella?"

"I'll give it to the priest."

"The towel?"

"That too."

Badla felt sorry. He had lost the opportunity to grab two new things.

"Father, who will eat all these?"

"Your grandfather, who else?"

"How? Will he come here from heaven? But heaven is so far away."

"Everybody comes here when they feel hungry." After they left, Badla pulled himself out like a tortoise from the tall weeds in which he had been hiding. His eyes shone brightly. Putli was waiting for rice. Badla's heart beat faster. Putli would give him everything. Panchu Ghosh and his son were far away. Badla started crawling as there was no other way. Scared that someone might spot him there, Badla could not even walk with his head held high. He could hear the sound of the gentle night breeze blowing.

On reaching the fen, Badla found that a lamp was still burning. The flame danced to the music of the night wind. A small insect was also dancing, intoxicated by the glare of the light. Badla remembered that Putli's eyes had the sharpness of a sword. She had raised in him a restless passion before vanishing around the corner.

Badla found it difficult to crawl any further. The day had been tiring and so full of tension. Going a bit further, he saw the food lying exactly as Panchu Ghosh had served it for his father. Badla imagined Putli eating the rice and speaking to him lovingly. He could not wait any longer. He wanted to take everything and run to Putli so that he could fondle her to his heart's content.

In the light of the lamp, Badla saw a fish head. Haro Ghosh must have loved to eat it. Badla liked it too but he suppressed his greed and decided to keep it for Putli. She said very often that a childless woman can be blessed with a child if she ate the head of a fish. Strange words, strange justification. Yet Badla felt excited. Putli's body was so soft and tender, her gait so easy and relaxed—all his reserve melted on seeing her. Looking at the heap of rice, Badla saw only Putli, her dreamy eyes and her naked hips.

There was no more time to waste. Badla picked up the meal for the dead with great care and held it close to his heart. The banana leaf produced a rustling sound. Some of the broth spilled on him. Like a heron hunting for fish, Badla looked around and drew in a deep breath. He saw the desolate fen, the fishermen's huts, and the lamps flickering in their shacks. He had seen such a light in Putli's eyes. Looking at that faraway star shining low and gentle, Badla felt after a long, long time that the world belonged to him.

Translated by Anuradha Sen

THE ALMOND FLOWERS

Buduram had no peace or happiness. Girls became old at the age of twenty, and here his only daughter Habhati was already nineteen. She had grown up so quickly. That she had a beautiful body, symmetrical and shapely, filled Buduram with fear and worry. Even in this intense cold the almond tree was covered with bright red flowers. Little bunches of flowers and buds filled the tree. Habhati was like the green grass—full of youth and vitality. She went to the woods every day to collect firewood and dry twigs. The border police looked at her with lustful eyes. But Habhati was not scared. If they tried to touch her, she would run away towards the dam like a deer.

Buduram's house with its pentile roof was close to the dam. In front of the house, the shade of the almond tree lay sprawled like a senseless man. Buduram lay on his charpoy in the calm shade twisting his thin hair around his finger, thinking about the future and the past.

His face was marked by care and worry: his forehead broadened as his hairline receded, his skin that was once smooth was now full of wrinkles, and his pointed chin made him look so ugly. When the winter ends he would go to the neighbouring villages. If he searched ten villages, he would surely find a suitable groom for his daughter Habhati. Till then, Buduram would have to put up with worry and anxiety. How would he even think about his home—a home that had no food? In the front, there lay about ten *cottas* of land like a barren woman. It was better that he did not look at it. Like every year, the rains had set in this year too. The land surrounded by the hills was covered with water. And what was the result? The produce from the fields was very scanty. It was not even sufficient for two months. When the earth struck, the wound did not heal easily. The wounds inflicted by the earth were too severe—Buduram was yet to recover from the attack. The worry that he had nothing to eat made him even older. Had he been alone, he would have begged and borrowed. But his daughter with her blossoming youth posed the greatest problem. Habhati could not go anywhere to work. Everybody was too attentive—not towards her work but towards her body. She returned home and wailed, "Father, I will not go anymore. If you have nothing to eat, nobody says anything. But if you end up with a venereal disease, people speak badly of you."

Earlier, Habhati used to make cane baskets. She used to cover six miles on foot to sell the baskets at the weekly market. She used to get firewood from the jungles which she carried on her head and sold in the town. Now everything had stopped. The forest department had put up a fence to stop the entry of men and animals. If they entered, the forest guards troubled them. That is why Habhati did not like to go there. She said that even being touched by those wicked people would ruin her whole life. "If I have to die, I will die at home, but I will not go there."

Since then all business had stopped. These days she gathered dry leaves from the roadside and at the most went with her friends to fetch water from the tube well. The rest of the time she remained at home. Her idle mind grew older slowly and steadily.

Early in the morning, the rays of the sun spread over the branches of the almond tree. Along with the ten cottas of land, this tree was also his property. At the time of his daughter's marriage, Buduram would sell this tree provided he got a good round sum for it. In these areas, the prices of wood and wheat were not the same. Every house had wood to spare. The sub-contractor's men came and bought it. Buduram sat on the charpoy, lost in thought. The sunlight that reached him through the branches bothered him. When the wind blew, the smell of the flowers made him feel giddy.

He had made up his mind to sell the tree. But Habhati did not like the idea. She had spoken in favour of the tree in elaborate detail and with innumerable humble entreaties, "Father, the tree does not ask for food or clothes. Why give it trouble? Let it remain as it is. Would a human being give you such cool shade in the summer?" Habhati had not said anything wrong. But the greedy earth did not take into account good or bad, right or wrong. Buduram looked around and stretched his body to shake off his lethargy. His eyes fell on the land. Barren and sterile, the land filled him with anger and he growled, "I will sell you, bitch, I will. What use is that smooth, bright body of yours to me? After spending so many hours on you, I get only two bags of rice. You think I can be satisfied with it? I am not such a man."

Buduram's anger increased as the day grew warmer. He removed the blanket and tried to stand up straight. He could feel a pain in his waist and his spine—a sharp, piercing pain like the sting of a bumblebee. He cried out in pain and then abused his old age and his bad luck. At times he even desired his daughter's death. His wife had died in childbirth at the time of delivery but the girl lived. People said that the daughter who had killed her mother would kill everything, everybody.

Buduram remembered the hard times. It was the year of the famine. The fierce heat that had come down the slopes of the mountains had burnt everything. The land had turned as black as soot. There had been no rice, no millet, no coarse wheat. The midwife had advised Buduram to name his daughter 'Lakshmi'.

This cruel joke hurt Buduram to his very core. As it is, he was going through a severe ordeal, plagued as he was by the sudden death of his wife and the famine. Since that day, it was not Lakshmi but 'Habhati', the wretched one, that his daughter came to be known as.

Habhati grew up like the other girls and, as the wretched one, did all the household chores. Standing under the shade of the almond tree, she wiped her face with the edge of her saree and then said, "O father, there is nothing—not even a morsel of food today. Go to the village and sell this old goat. Otherwise we won't have anything to fill our stomachs with." That was not a bad idea, Buduram thought. He had pawned nearly everything to the grocer, there was nothing left. Moreover, the old goat had loose motion. But it could still walk. So if he did not sell it now, both the goat and the money would be lost. Buduram stood up straight in fear. He had to cover a long distance before the sun became stronger, otherwise there was trouble in store for him. A big bowl of rice beer with onion and green chilli refreshed and reinvigorated Buduram. Calling out to his daughter, he said, "You don't have to sweep the leaves. Tie the goat. Let's see what fortune has in store for me today."

Buduram set out, in one hand a walking stick to support his bent, feeble body and in the other the rope to which the goat was tied. He went slowly towards the checkpost. Habhati watched the frail figure of her father, bent from the waist. She heaved a sigh and looked up at the sky. How beautiful it looked! The glorious colours and the splendour of the early morning sent her into a dizzy rapture.

Habhati felt that the winter sky spoke of love. No sooner did the thought cross her mind than she felt her blood rising in waves in her veins. In the narrow valley between her heavy breasts, sweat flowed like a river. Blood from her feet came up to redden her cheeks. Her face glowed. It looked redder than the red petals of the almond flowers. Habhati could not stand there any longer. She threw the broom and ran inside.

Habhati could not remain in the empty room. Her mind could not stand the emptiness. It was all her fault. She had no need to go to the checkpost to fetch water. Now it was too late. She was very sure that Sepoybabu was an enchanter. She was under his magic spell, or else, why should she feel so restless? Why should she feel so deeply for this man, a foreigner? The man knew magic; his eyes were pools into which Habhati had dived only to be drowned. She did not know how to swim, so she frantically struggled to escape the depths. She did not know how to search for ways to be rescued. It was as if Sepoybabu had caught her with a fish hook and was pulling her towards him. Habhati trembled in fear and looked out. The trucks that speeded past produced different sounds. Habhati shuddered on hearing the sounds. She felt her heart quicken and her blood ran cold.

He did not listen. He did not care to listen even when she tried to stop him. He was like the tempestuous storm that was ready to blow her away. It ignited strange warm feelings within her. It was like she was in a delicious delirium. How could she stop him? His musk became one with the strong perfume of the almond flowers and kept her comatose. Habhati was lost in thought. She passed her fingers through her hair and drew out dirt. She felt nauseous on seeing it and turned her eyes towards the jungle at the border. It was so dense even in the winter. The trees were clothed in different shades of green. When the wind blew, the trees spoke in whispers. Yet the almond tree had shed all its leaves at the very outset of winter. It stood naked as though it wished to be amorous, to love and fondle, to make love to the bare sky. She could not accept this repulsive greediness. Was physical consummation really so important? Did love then demand only the flesh? Is it all just physical? Is it not a spontaneous merging of two bodies who are also soulmates?

Fixing her saree, she looked sternly at the tree. The branches and twigs were covered with buds. Habhati could not turn her eyes away from the dark crimson-coloured buds.

The fire warmed her body from deep within. Drops of sweat covered her beautiful face. In the moonlit night, standing under the almond tree, Sepoybabu had touched her hands lightly. That night too, beads of perspiration had covered Habhati's hands and face. Sepoybabu had said, "How can 'Habhati' be a name? Your name is Phool because you are beautiful, bright and full of ardour like the almond flowers. I will call you Phool."

Nobody had said such words to her before. Everybody had wanted to take her into the dense jungle for hunting—hunting only her body. Since that day, she had been drawn towards him, and unless she saw him, she had no peace.

She went to the checkpost very often on the pretext of fetching water. He was always there. The moment he heard the harsh sounds of the tube well, he opened the window and looked at her with unblinking eyes. Habhati had never met or seen anyone like him. And whenever she thought of him as her own, she felt so terribly scared. She felt that she was asking for the impossible. She was perhaps running after the kind of happiness which was not for her, which was an illusion. Yet she was completely entranced. Had it not been for her old father, the barriers would have broken down and Habhati would have then warmed herself in the heat of another body. She could not bring herself to do what her friends did so casually. When the buds blossomed into flowers, it would be time for the wedding. Then he would ask for Habhati's hand. Before that, it would only be fond looks, a small caress, or a slight touch, chaste and pure.

Her friend Shanichari worked as a labourer with the sub-contractor. She had gone with him to the riverside to work at the mine. Now Shanichari was pregnant. All the herbs and roots that the midwife had given her to cause an abortion had failed. She was big with child and there was extensive public censure and hooting. Shanichari could only lament, "I don't want to live. I will take poison. Men are like venomous serpents. How can I save myself from their fangs?"

Habhati felt terribly scared whenever she looked at Shanichari. At such moments she did not wish to see the almond tree. She tossed and turned on the charpoy. She understood that girls had to put up with hundreds of troubles. The night bird was calling its mate; the night sky stayed awake with the stars and so did Habhati. How could she sleep? She stared at the pentile roof and watched in silence the playful tricks of winter. One thought, however, haunted her—if Sepoybabu came to her on such a calm tranquil night when the heart longed to be with its beloved, would she send him back?

Habhati sighed. Shanichari's child was playing in the room. Habhati hugged the child and spoke lovingly. Her loving words filled the room. Sepoybabu had gone to his native village. His mother was seriously ill; she would not survive. Habhati felt sad and scared. Everything was out of her hands. For the past few days, she had been drawing lines on the wall with charcoal to keep account of the days. The wall was full of lines, yet there was no sign of Sepoybabu. So many trucks and buses passed by and then stopped at the checkpost. So many people alighted, so many boarded the bus—but where was her babu? Her tears dried up as time passed and dawn became dusk.

Sepoybabu had met her before he left. There was nothing and nobody in the woods except a breeze and the birds. The breath of the two humans became the breath of the forest, their admiring glances like the branches of two trees swaying to touch one another, gently, lovingly. Taking both her hands in his, Sepoybabu had told her, "Do not worry. Take care. I will return soon. See, it is time for the tree to shed its leaves; before I come back, it will surely cover itself with flowers once more. We will meet again then."

Habhati was silent. She had no strength left to utter even a word. She gazed at the tree that had shaken off its leaves. Right then a gust of moaning wind dashed against the sal tree. Habhati trembled and moved close to Sepoybabu. He pulled her closer, the warmth of his body flooding over her. It was so beautiful, so dear that she held it sacred.

Sepoybabu had told her, "The almond tree has been a witness to our love. Look at the tree. In every flower you will find me and my fragrance. And I will find you."

Habhati listened to him in wonder. He said, "The tree cannot be an ordinary tree. Standing in its shade we can look up to see the clear blue sky. It is our duty to save the tree from all attacks."

Today too Habhati drew a line with the charcoal. She felt sad; she could not concentrate on any work. The land and the trees were singed and so was her mind. She longed for a cool breeze, a soothing touch, but where would she find that in this intense heat? She stared vacantly at the brown land and burst out crying. The almond tree was so confident of itself. It had covered its branches with buds. Habhati tried to control herself but she could not. All of a sudden she saw the ugly crows on the branches, tearing and eating the flowers with their sharp, pointed beaks. Habhati rushed out in anger. She picked up a big stone and threw it at the crows. They flew away only to return again. Habhati stared helplessly at the broken petals that lay scattered. She broke down completely.

Buduram returned in the evening when the sun had thrown a pale curtain over the fields and meadows. Habhati was worn out with tension, sorrow and hunger. Seeing her father, her face lit up. *How weak and feeble men become as they grow old!* thought Habhati. How long would her father live? Only the other day he fell down while returning from the market. Thank God, there were people around and so he could be saved. Her father could not see clearly. So, he fell asleep early in the evening. How could he sleep so soundly when he had so many worries? It was for her that her father had no peace. It was for her that he was bent double. Whatever strength of body and mind he had was taken away by constant worry and anxiety for the land. If the land showed no sympathy, there would be no end to their troubles and sorrows. But Buduram did not believe this. He believed that the land could never harm them. It would, on the contrary, make them rich and prosperous. Her old father always said that without water and manure, how could the land give them any crop?

Habhati listened in silence. They had no cattle. Where would the manure come from? At times her father would vent his anger upon the land. He called it a blood-sucking devil. Or else wouldn't he get some produce at least?

Buduram sat comfortably on the charpoy for some time. Then he washed his hands and face and looked at Habhati. His eyes seemed to tell her that she would not have to endure any more sorrow. She should cook and eat and be merry.

Habhati could not understand the reason for such joy. Was there any special news which had filled her father with such delight? Buduram laughed and said, "Daughter, there is God. He has heard me. Otherwise, why would they come now?" Habhati could not understand anything. Buduram sat on the charpoy swinging his legs happily.

Night fell. Habhati kept staring at the faraway light. Her eyes pained. Buduram was restless. He too looked towards the road but nothing could be seen. Habhati could not suppress her curiosity. She said, "What are you staring at? Tell me."

Buduram started coughing. Then after some time he said, "See if anybody is coming. I cannot see, my eyes are paining."

"Who will come?"

Buduram smiled. He looked brighter, and younger too. Like a healthy, strong person, he said, "The men with their sheep. I met them at the weekly market. They said that they would come here, to our village. The deal is closed. The whole night the sheep will graze in the field, and I will bear the expenses of the three in the group."

"What will you gain?"

Buduram laughed at his daughter's ignorance. If a hundred and twenty sheep relieved themselves in the field, there was no need for any more manure. The land will be fortified. It would provide them with a rich harvest. There would be no problem, no worry for another ten years.

Last year the men had been to Sukrain's land. The village had crowded there. Habhati too went with Shanichari. Never before had she seen so many sheep. Shanichari said to her after sometime, "Let's go home. The *pardeshis* know many tricks, their eyes are full of lust." Habhati did not pay much attention to Shanichari's words. Today she felt faint in apprehension of an unknown fear.

Buduram was busy. He asked Habhati to cook meat with chilli and spices. The babus were pardeshis. They liked their food rich, with spices. Habhati nodded. Her father said, "They are three. They said that they have not tasted meat in a long time. So..."

Habhati said nothing. Then she saw blood under the almond tree that made her tremble in fear. His father had grown old but had still not become sensible. She could not look at the tree; she felt guilty. Sepoybabu had asked her to look after the tree. No sin should ever touch it.

With a heavy heart Habhati did her work. Then she shook her father who sat dozing and said, "Go, father, give them the food. It is ready."

"Why don't you go, daughter?" Buduram yawned.

Habhati kept quiet. She knew her father could not see properly. She did not waste any more time. She took the chapatis and meat and went towards the jungle. In the moonlit night, she could see everything clearly.

She stopped under the *kadam* tree to remove a thorny creeper. The bushes were covered with small white flowers and dry yellow leaves lay on the zig-zag path. The leaves crunched and the twigs snapped as she walked over them. The sound was familiar yet it produced fear.

Habhati wrapped her saree carefully around her bare shoulders. She was not scared. Winter would last only two months before it was summer again. The almond tree would be covered with green leaves once more. There would be no sorrow in the world, and Buduram would plough his fields. What could be better than that? A nearly dead man would slowly grow strong and healthy again.

Habhati walked quickly. Suddenly the lamp went out. A strong hairy hand pulled her into the bushes. She tried to scream but could not. The wind carried a faint groan, barely audible. A cicada flew away in fear. A fox moved around and saw everything. It had sharp nails, yet it did nothing.

Habhati's saree flapped in the wind. She tried to wrap it around her body but failed. She fell at the feet of the strong and hefty man. He did not push her away. In a cold and indifferent voice, "Your father wanted manure, so I gave it. Go back home. There will be crops."

The man took the container with the food and walked towards the fields. He turned back and said, "If you speak about this, I will kill you. Go home."

Then the man went away. There was no fragrance in the breeze. Habhati could not walk, she could not breathe. She vomited and cried as she reached the almond tree. The flowers fell down one by one. Habhati could only stare at them.

Another day, bright and beautiful like any other. Dewdrops sparkled on the green grass that covered the land. Flowers looked at the sun with pale eyes.

Habhati could not sleep. She could not even lie down. With an axe in hand, she paced the floor. She did not eat. She only drank three bowls of rice beer that cold night. Yet her desire for revenge had not abated.

In the middle of the night, Habhati came to the almond tree. She had to come. The red light of the checkpost was flickering. Fear crawled all over her body like a worm. She could not stay there for long. She could not endure the red light, like red eyes looking at her. She came back crying.

Buduram had left the cosy shelter of his house with the early rays of the crimson sun. He came back along with the hundred and twenty sheep and called out to her, "Daughter, bring the pole. The babus are going away." Frightened, Habhati came outside. She could not look up. Her whole body burnt in shame and humiliation and she looked pale and wan.

Buduram said again,"Go bring the pole. I will sell the flowers for thirty rupees. It is all right, is it not?"

Habhati was dumbfounded. Buduram brought down the pole from the roof. Then looking at her he said, "Go get the flowers. I am an old man. I have no more strength left."

Habhati looked around, sad and dismayed. She looked strangely at the tree. She would not cry, not in front of everybody. She gulped and looked at her father again. He tried to make her understand, "These are wild flowers. They have no smell, nothing! Of what use are they? Give them to the babus, they will be pleased." Habhati broke branch after branch full of the red flowers. The young man laughed. The smell of burnt bidi floated in the air.

When Sepoybabu returned, there was not a single flower left. Looking at the tree bereft of flowers and leaves, stripped of its beauty, he could not see their sky. He could not see the Elysian sky. He only saw Habhati sobbing. Her face was red, like an almond flower soaked in dew.

Translated by Anuradha Sen

THE CHOWKIDAR

Sanatan, the village chowkidar, looked crestfallen. Strong and well built, he was in his mid-fifties though he looked hardly forty. He had been the leader of a gang of skilled stick fighters; now he was the watchman for Area Number 7. The village people called him Sana Chowkidar. He was responsible for the safety of the village. His heavy steps echoed in the lanes and by-lanes. Every night he stayed awake.

It was perhaps for this reason that he had developed severe stomach problems. Sanatan knew very well that his night duty was at the root of it. It was for these stomach problems that his hair turned grey so early, and his beard thinned away which made him look old. He had a place to stay but there was no one to look after it. His wife Sushama did not like Sanatan staying out all night on duty. All fire and passion, she found it difficult to stay alone. She ran away with another man leaving behind her three-year-old son, Bishu.

The same Bishu, now known as Biswanath, had joined college. He liked to stay away from the village. Sometimes he wrote to his father. Those letters gave Sanatan a much longed-for shelter, a support in his old age. Bishu was not like the other boys of his age. Always a good student, he had scored high marks in the school-leaving examination and secured a scholarship to attend college for free. He was one in a million. Bishu had a very good memory. He remembered everything—nothing ever slipped his mind. Sanatan had been quite happy with his wife and son. It was Sushama's elopement that severed the thread of happiness from his life. Bishu was the only link with the past that Sanatan wanted to forget. Yet strangely and sadly enough, this link that had offered him solace wanted to sever all ties. Sanatan was sad.

The officer-in-charge sent for him the other day and rebuked him for negligence in duty. Sanatan did not know what to say. It was as if someone had poured boiling oil in his ears. He wished he had died before hearing such words, before being branded as a man of ill repute. He could not make the officer understand anything. The officer was a strict man and he stuck to his views. Sanatan returned with a heavy heart. As it is he was overcome by sorrow and grief about something that was very personal. It was nearly three months since Bishu had written to him. The boy did not bother to write even a line or two to his father. He had always been an introvert and so it was difficult for Sanatan to understand his ways. The father and the son never shared their joys and sorrows. Each sat alone, lost in his own thoughts. On such occasions, Sanatan's feelings were hurt. He had never expected such undesirable behaviour from Bishu, his only son. Bishu's attitude made it hard for Sanatan to speak to his son about his sorrows. He suppressed his grief and suffered, and Bishu had no knowledge of this. As days passed, the distance between father and son grew slowly and silently, till one day they became total strangers.

Halodharbabu, the chief of the *panchayat,* was the only man in Area Number 7 who had a gun. He had a two-storeyed house, a mango grove and about a hundred acres of land. Sanatan had to meet him in the morning. He decided to set out after having a cup of tea. But he was startled by the colour of the tea—it looked as red as human blood. He drank tea every morning but never had such thoughts come to his mind before.

He felt uneasy and agitated. As he stared into the distance, Bishu's face appeared upon the canvas of his mind. Sanatan longed to see him once; it had been three months since he last saw his son. He had no idea where Bishu was or how he was. He was told that his son had left the college hostel. That he was involved in some violent political strife and the police were after him. They had enough evidence that bore out the allegations. Sanatan could not ignore Madhav or the information he provided. He had never understood Bishu; his attitude was so fiery that it put Sanatan on his guard almost immediately.

Sanatan could not finish the tea. He threw it away. For the past few days, he had been feeling disturbed and had a premonition of some danger. He never thought of his wife but his son was dear to him. Day and night, Sanatan was occupied with his own daily needs. In spite of that, he missed his son very much. Last night he had been wide awake. He could have slept after the first call of the rooster. But he did not. He had a terrible headache and he felt a pain in his chest. Gripping his stick firmly in his hand, he reflected about his past. His wife Sushama had married again. Her second husband was a bus conductor. And she had joined a *jatra* party as a dancer. One day he had seen her at the weekly market. He had recognised her immediately. But Sushama did not acknowledge him. There were dark circles under her eyes and no sign of either happiness or gratification. Sushama's face flashed in his mind's eye on dark and silent nights. Bishu never spoke about his mother. To him, she was sheer poison, a symbol of bad luck. Ruminating over unfortunate details only added to one's pain. How much sorrow can a man endure in one lifetime?

Sanatan sighed and then started walking, firmly gripping his stick. The stick was his strength, his friend; it was the magic wand and the symbol of his duty. The stick knew that he had never evaded his responsibilities. It was not in his nature to do so. He believed that those who tried to deceive others were themselves deceived in the long run. Life was sacred to him and work, worship. In this holy setup, Sanatan considered himself to be rather insignificant. But he wished to make others understand that one can have control over one's life. Old Kami used to be a thief once and every night, while on duty, Sanatan met him. Kami used to massage oil all over his body and then set out in the darkness of the night with a tool that he used to break into houses. If their eyes met, he would smile a wan smile and say, "Please don't mind. I am a thief, and you are a night-guard. Our work and our paths are different. I will not go by the way you go. Who knows—we might bump against each other in the dark and hit our heads. In the dark, the thief and the guard are one and the same." The same Kami now sold potatoes in the local market. He had flung his tool away deep into the pond. He told Sanatan very often, "You are the philosopher's stone, and I am rusted iron. Your touch has transformed me into gold. God will be good to you."

Sanatan came out of his hut. He had a sudden indisposition to action. He wanted to rest, to sleep, but there was no time for it. He had to go to the office; he could not disregard Halodharbabu's order. He crossed the main road and stood under the shade of a neem tree. It was a hot, windless day and the bright sun was a torture. People had no relief and their condition was as pitiable as the trees that were drying up. They looked up at the sky, hoping for rain since they were all farmers and without rain, they were helpless. Even in the month of Baisakh, the land was cracked, but still the clear blue sky had no mercy. Sanatan left the main road and walked along the unmetalled road so that he could walk under the shade of the trees. Madhav's house was in the centre of the village. If he went there, perhaps he could get some information about Bishu. He shook off the lazy feeling and walked quickly. He met Benubabu on the way, who said to Sanatan, "What is the matter? Where are you going in such a hurry?"

Sanatan paused. Then wiping the sweat from his face he said, "Halodharbabu sent for me, so I am going to meet him, Babu. Bishu has not come home in so many days. I feel sad. Every now and then I think about him. I do not know what I should do."

"Why don't you go and meet him once?"

Sanatan sighed. "I long to go but it means added expenditure. The bus fare is twenty rupees. With tea and food, it will come to thirty rupees. Where will I get the money from? So, I am sitting quietly. Let me see if he writes."

Benubabu cared for Sanatan. He tried to reassure him, "Don't worry. Have faith in God, he will settle everything. Still, if you feel very sad, then go and visit him. I will give you the money."

Sanatan hesitated. He was so grateful to Benubabu. Yet during times of trouble, Sanatan could not stand by him. Halodharbabu did not let him. Benubabu had no children. His landed property provided enough for a square meal. But somehow or the other he got involved in troubles.

Benubabu had a black ox. He had dedicated it to Lord Shiva and set it free for public welfare. This black ox had become a source of terror. It destroyed the harvest, chased young girls and maidens to breathlessness, and if its eyes fell on the pits and ditches, then nobody could stop it from going in. This was not all. It was no less intelligent than a man. It never harmed Benubabu; all its anger was directed towards the evil and the wicked of the village. Halodharbabu's eldest daughter was going to college one day. The ox saw her red scarf and chased her for about a mile. Running scared, the girl finally tumbled and fell into the catkin bushes. Her red scarf went flying towards the faraway rice fields. The black ox did not stop even for a moment. It followed the red scarf with tenacity and reached the rice fields. It harassed the people and spoiled the crop. Having utterly disrupted everything, it vanished. The reckless damage was a trivial matter for Halodharbabu. Much more important to him was his daughter and her fracture. Her leg had to be put in a plaster cast and the village doctor visited twice. This incident had wiped the smile off Halodharbabu's face. Even his enemies would have been filled with pity on seeing his pale, withered face.

Benubabu was innocent, yet Halodharbabu held him responsible for the events that took place. One afternoon, he abused Benubabu and warned him, "The ox is yours and you must keep it in check. I have never seen such a killer. It is disrupting peace in the village. I am the Panchayat—do you think I will allow myself to be rendered powerless and be a puppet like Jagannath, the handless deity of Puri? I tell you once and for all: I will not tolerate such indecent, abominable practice."

The black ox dedicated to Lord Shiva was free to roam and ramble as it liked; it was not to be kept bound. There was no place for it in the cowsheds, for it could not be considered an equal of the stray cattle. The owner of the shed said, "I cannot give up my religion for business. The ox belongs to the Lord. Do you think I am so strong that I can tie down the ox that belongs to the Lord?"

Halodharbabu grimaced. Grinding his teeth, he said, "I know that very well. But it can't be excused every time. If an offender is punished after each and every offence that it commits, then the ox should be punished too."

The village folk were amazed to hear the verdict of the local chief. A blow to religion? No, it cannot be accepted. The wisest among them all said, "Who does not know that the Hindus worship the cow in true faith? This is a practice in each and every house. How can we stop the ox? Only death can put a stop to it. But who will bell the cat? Who is so strong and bold and powerful?" Everybody looked at Halodharbabu, the panacea for all ills. And indeed he was. Halodharbabu had ten ploughs and one gun. How could an ox stand a chance against a gun? It would be blown away like a leaf in a storm. Everybody surrounded him. They said, "The ox has harmed you the most. So you should kill it. Moreover, you have a gun. Just pull the trigger once and that will finish the ox and all its pranks."

A heroic deed, yet Halodharbabu shrank back in fear. He did have a gun, but would he pick up a gun to kill the ox? Such a shameful thought! These days some Hindus slaughtered cows and ate beef—did he too belong to that group? O God! The holy thread he wore as a Brahmin stretched from his right shoulder to his waist, like a river etched out on a map. He did not put a morsel in his mouth before chanting a series of prayers while counting beads on a rosary. He gave an annual donation of a hundred and one rupees to the temple of Sri Chaitanya. When it did not rain, the Vaishnavas gathered in his courtyard, which was swabbed and purified with cow dung solution, chanting 'Hare Krishna, Hare Rama' to the rhythm of *kartal* and *khol*. Being such a noble and religious man, how could he ever commit such a deadly sin?

The meeting ended and the people called in Sanatan Chowkidar. He was rebuked severely and reminded sternly that it was his duty to save the village. If what had been taking place fell under his responsibilities, then it was high time that he cast away the government-issued livery. He should rather wear a dhoti, and wander more and eat less.

One day the black ox went and destroyed the Panchayat office. While going out, it smashed the signboard into pieces. Halodharbabu covered his nose as he smelled the strong, pungent odour of the animal's dung. He said, "This is too much, I cannot tolerate such unholy practice." He ordered Sanatan, "Call Benubabu. Call him immediately. What does he think of himself? Will he incite the ox to defeat us in the election? No chance! I will do something."

Benubabu supported another political party. His views naturally did not accord with Halodharbabu's. He was totally indifferent about this matter. On being pressed, he said, "I have dedicated it to the Lord. He will keep it in check. What is the use of harassing me? I am a simple man. I do not understand anything about ox politics."

Halodharbabu's temper knew no bounds. Yet, he had to control his feelings. After all, he was a gentleman. Meanwhile, Madhav met Sanatan and informed him about Bishu, "I do not understand your son's ways or what he does. He did not sit for the examination. He lost his temper when I told him to come home with me. He said that his blood boiled every time he came here. He could not tolerate the injustice; it was difficult for him to remain silent. So he did not come. He also said that he had work to do—political work—and he had to complete it. When I asked him about you, he laughed. He said that you were fine. As long as Halodharbabu was here, you would be hale and hearty. His words were full of anger. I could not speak to him for long."

It was as if a hot wave had scorched Sanatan. An abysmal void filled his entire being. He had never thought that his own son would go so far away from him. The hope he had nurtured crumbled in front of his eyes. Looking at Madhav's innocent, simple face, his sorrows doubled. Madhav and Bishu were childhood friends. Always together. How would he know that one of the two would be utterly ruined?

Madhav tried to console him, "Don't feel so sad. Bishu is involved in politics but he is clean. I cannot begin to tell you how helpful he is. He has no enemy."

But Sanatan would not be comforted so easily. He had not brought up Bishu with such love and care only for this. The boy, whose father spent sleepless nights for want of food, had no right to indulge in such luxury. Sanatan hated politics. It was nothing but a disease in his opinion. He did not even like to cast his vote in favour of anyone. What was the use? There would be no change in his life or in the lives of others like him. Sanatan would spit on politics that did not want the good of the country or its people.

The officer had told him that a chowkidar's eyes should be like those of a vulture and his ears like a dog's. He should be as cunning as a fox and, of course, very strong. If not, then he should give up the job. Sanatan had felt scared. Then boldly he had replied, "Babu, till date I have not earned a bad name. The officers have always been pleased with my work. They have rewarded me. I have a certificate too. I can show it to you tomorrow."

"There's no need for it. If you are so capable, then catch those who are scribbling slogans on the walls." The officer looked worried. Sanatan understood that somebody had written slogans, spilling blood on the walls of the school building. Fiery, thought-provoking words adorned the school walls. The O.C. had seen all this; Halodharbabu had seen it too. Sanatan had accompanied them. He did not know that words could fill one with such fear. Halodharbabu said that as if fear of the black ox was not enough, the slogans had to join hands with it. The officer then narrated how his colleague was stabbed to death in town by two young men. If the policemen were attacked, then there would be disorder everywhere. He said emphatically, "This is a political murder. We are looking for the group behind it. If we can catch them, we will skin them alive." Then looking at the walls, he continued, "This is not a good sign. All this must be nipped in the bud, else it will become a burden. Well, Halodharbabu, do you doubt anyone?"

"It is all Benubabu's doing," hissed Halodharbabu. "He is not a good man. He is crooked. He has all the young boys under his control."

After this, the police jeep went directly to Benubabu's house. All his papers, letters, diary and other documents were seized by the police. Flushing with joy, Halodharbabu committed an evil deed. He killed two innocent monkeys with his gun. Their fault? They had broken a branch from his mango tree and had wasted the unripe mangoes. So they had to be killed. But the rest of the gang did not appreciate Halodharbabu's cruelty. Their cries and lamentation brought tears to the eyes of the onlookers. Sanatan was called. He pulled the dead creatures away from there. Halodharbabu gave him two rupees as reward. That day, while drinking tea, Sanatan again saw blood in his cup.

Benubabu was not guilty. The police acquitted him of the charges brought against him. Halodharbabu was happy that his daughter could walk and play about again. The people, however, were still afraid of the ox. It could hide itself in the darkness of the night, carry out its frenzied act and then disappear from view. Nobody dared to do anything. A meeting was held again. Halodharbabu presided over the meeting where it was decided that the ox would be speared to death. If by chance it was caught, then a thin metal rod would be heated and then thrust into its eyes. Or a poisonous spear would be thrown to injure it.

What chance does an animal stand against the human brain? Kalu Sheikh had nursed his anger against the ox as it had destroyed his crops. He readily threw the spear which injured the ox badly. It was a head injury. The terrible cries of the ox filled the air as it sat down slowly on the ground. Its moaning brought tears to Sanatan's eyes. Nobody cared to listen to him.

Madhav said that there was a similarity between Bishu and the ox. Going near the ox in broad daylight raised clouds of criticism but there was no harm in going under the cover of the dark night. Halodharbabu went twice every day to see its condition and he cursed Benubabu each time. The news that the ox was in great pain had reached Benubabu. But he was helpless. He went to the veterinary surgeon and with hands folded in plea, he said, "Please save the ox. I cannot sit and watch an innocent creature dying. It is a sin. Please begin the treatment."

The vet's heart softened. He arrived with medicines and an injection. But he was not given the chance to do his work. Halodharbabu said to him, "I do admire your concern but you will not be allowed to go to the ox. Where the interest of the entire village is at stake, you cannot exercise your might. Please go back."

The surgeon went back and the ox fought with death. It could not stand straight. The wound did not heal. It worsened day by day. Within seven days, the ox was just skin and bones. Worms and maggots crawled in the wound and flies buzzed around it all day long. Tears rolled from its eyes as it sat behind the Panchayat office. Its days were numbered.

Benubabu came to Sanatan one night. There was a lost look in those eyes. With fear Sanatan said, "What is the matter?"

Benubabu looked at him. He did not know how to put forward the suggestion. Then after some time, he said, "I have come to you to ask for help. I know only you can help me in my trouble."

Sanatan hesitated. Then he said, "Yes, Babu. What can I do for you?"

Benubabu informed him in a low voice about his wife who had stopped drinking even water. How could she when her child could not? And she had been crying day and night. Couldn't Sanatan go and give some oil cake and water to the ox? It had been without food for seven days. "We have no children, the ox is everything to us," Benubabu wiped his tears and said that he too could endure no more. If it went and died somewhere else, then they wouldn't have felt so sad. Death is inevitable anyway.

Sanatan looked at Benubabu for a long time. Then he said, "Babu, I have something to say in this matter, if you don't mind." Benubabu looked up with questioning eyes. Sanatan said, "I will take the ox away tonight and leave it at my relative's place. They would look after it and provide the necessary treatment."

It was quite late at night. Sanatan had brought the ox from the village and was guiding it lovingly along the way.

"Come, my dear. Come. Here, we have nearly reached. Just a little more to go! Walk a bit faster, come on..."

The poor ox could not walk. It fell down again and again. It had no strength left. If it bent its head, blood flowed out from the open wound. The flies did not bother it as it was night-time.

Sanatan stroked its body gently and said again, "Come, walk a bit faster. If we are caught, they will skin me alive. Do you want that?"

The ox walked with unsteady steps. In its desire to live, it became desperate. Sanatan had avoided the main road and was going along the field. It was lined with trees and bushes.

The silence of the night was broken by Sanatan's words and the laboured grunts of the ox. Then, in an attempt to run, the ox stumbled and fell. Sanatan nearly cried out in anguish. He sat down beside the ox urging it with loving words to get up. The delay might cost him heavily. Suddenly, his eyes fell on the carrion around him and he shuddered in fear.

Around the bend came a jeep. The headlights drove away the darkness and the sound of the engine broke the silence of the night. A vulture came down from the treetop. It was a cloudy night. Sanatan stared at the jeep in surprise.

Four-five sepoys jumped out and asked, "Shall we drop the body here?"

"Yes, yes. Hurry up."

The O.C. remained alert. The sepoys carried the corpse. Blood was still oozing out from the body. Lighting a cigarette, the O.C. said, "You swine! You will write slogans, you will revolt, will you? Now lie here." The sepoys threw down the body. Then the jeep speeded away.

Sanatan lit a match and saw—it was Bishu's body lying on the ground just a few yards away from him. Blood was still gushing from his nose and mouth. Sanatan fell upon his son's body. Embracing his dead son, he cried out, "Bishu! O my son! Please speak to me once, just once."

It was nearly dawn. The vultures came down in huge numbers driven by hunger. Sanatan stood tall and straight between the two dead bodies. He was not afraid of the crows and the vultures. He would fight it out. He would die before he gave up his claim on the corpse.

Translated by Anuradha Sen

THE GANGMAN

Huts. Broken, crooked, sordid, dirty, rotten huts that fringed the railway tracks. An eye-sore. A crow sat cawing, its rough, unmusical voice shattering the peace and tranquility of the early morning.

It was summertime. The inmates of the huts had no respite from the suffocating heat even at night.

Old Iswar lay awake all night. His entire body bathed in sweat and covered with the dirt from the dirty bedding upon which he lay panting like a wounded animal. He felt terribly unhappy and all sorts of images came to his mind. He looked at his hand—its beauty marred because of the two fingers he had lost—and surging waves of grief crashed upon the shore of his mind. How could he endure the sorrow?

Iswar did not grieve or lament his missing fingers. He lamented over himself. At the dusk of his life, the old man was filled with grief and sorrow for his own self, neglected and insulted as he was by the authorities, his son and daughter-in-law, his neighbours.

Iswar's only son Kartik liked a life of luxury and comfort. So did Phelna, his wife, whom he had spoilt with affection. Phelna expressed displeasure at everything and was too vocal about her likes and dislikes. About Iswar too. Iswar had nothing much to say. With an annoyed look on his face, Kartik tried to reassure him at such moments.

"What are you so sad about? Only two fingers lost. Your life has been saved. Isn't that enough? And we are here with you. We will look after you." Kartik's words gave him strength that was only momentary.

These days, Kartik's words and behaviour brought clouds of doubt and disbelief to his mind. And this was only natural. Having married a girl from the slums, a girl as coarse as sack-cloth in Iswar's opinion, Kartik felt he was on top of the world. They spent their days rolling on the mat without a care in the world.

Iswar lost his fingers while changing the sleepers of the railway track. His severed fingers fell upon the gravel as Iswar writhed in pain. He felt an uncanny sensation before it all faded to black and Iswar, the gangman, fell down on the tracks, unconscious.

The other gangmen had taken him to the railway hospital where he was admitted. When he came to his senses, he was told that his blood had coloured the rough gravel and sand around the railway tracks red.

Iswar's accident filled the junior officer with irritation and anxiety. This was not because he was concerned with Iswar's safety but because of the injury-on-duty certificate that he had to issue.

"Look at that clumsy country lout! Always lost in his own thoughts," he exclaimed in anger. "And now the IOD!"

However, Birij Das, Iswar's literate young colleague, informed the officer that he had to issue the certificate. In a calm and composed manner, unruffled by the officer's outburst he said, "You have to issue the certificate, Sir. There is nothing undisclosed in Iswarda's case. You have nothing to feel nervous about in this matter."

The officer, however, was hardly comforted by Birij's words of assurance. He could not tolerate this dark lanky boy. An ill-tempered fellow, Birij was the leader of not just one gang but all twenty. A word or a glance from him and the gangmen would gladly give up their lives.

After having spent a full thirty days in hospital, Iswar returned home. Though his wound had not healed completely, the doctors had issued a fitness certificate.

Birij came to visit Iswar without fail every morning and evening. He tried his best to reassure Iswar who was completely disappointed and disillusioned. Over and over he said that Iswarda had nothing to worry about because all of them were with him in his hard times. "Take rest for a few more days, then come back to work," he advised.

Rest was not for Iswar. On the second day after his return from the hospital, he was called to the office. The senior officer tried to make Iswar understand that he had no leaves left.

"If you stay at home, Iswar, it would mean no payment. Do you understand? So don't you think you should resume duty immediately?" The officer's words sounded logical and reasonable. After all, what would he do sitting at home? He would only be chewing the cud.

Iswar's wife had died of dysentery a year back. Since then, he was alone. Nobody, not even his own son, had any time for him. He understood with great sorrow that his ability to pay the monthly subsistence was the beginning and end of the interest he inspired in his family. He wondered if this is how things ought to be. Heaving a deep sigh, Iswar tried to come to terms with himself, with life.

"This is how the world is," he said aloud. His son Kartik sold fruits in the railway market nearby. Iswar had taken out a loan from his provident fund for Kartik to set up his business. Still, neither Kartik nor his wife was happy. Every word they uttered, every step they took, every look they gave revealed the intense dissatisfaction they harboured in their hearts. Kartik went around hawking fruits with his cart in the scorching heat. His wife applied a soothing, fragrant powder on the prickly heat rash every afternoon. But it could not mask the stale odour that had taken possession of her mind and soul. She did not bother to keep her voice low as she spoke to Kartik, poisoning his mind against his old father. Some of her biting remarks reached Iswar and left a permanent mark on his mind.

"Your father is a leech. He will stick to us and suck our blood. Why can't he die?"

Iswar remained silent even after such attacks. Like an overladen ass, he patiently suffered all that came upon him through no fault of his. The son looked on as the daughter-in-law raged.

Phelna began her day cursing Iswar, grudging even the glass of tea which she offered him with sheer disgust and neglect. The old man was anguished having to live like an unwelcome guest in his own house. Despised by his daughter-in-law and slighted on every little occasion, he looked at the glass tumbler and felt it was not tea that she had served but his own red blood. He had never felt like this before. It was a worn-out relation held together by necessity only, and nothing more. Looking at his daughter-in-law, six months' pregnant, Iswar did not experience the thrilling sensation that ought to have flowed in the veins of a would-be grandfather.

Kartik pampered Phelna a lot. It was perhaps for this that she dared to ill-treat Iswar. But didn't she know that had it not been for him, she and her husband would have starved to death? Not to mention the luxuries.

Iswar sipped the tea. He could not shake off the drowsiness. He belched. It must be acute indigestion, he thought. The chapatis that Phelna had served him the previous night were too dry and hard for his old jaws. As for the meals that she cooked, thought Iswar, it was better to remain silent. He always ate what was served to him without a word. If he expressed annoyance at the food served, his daughter-in-law would not keep her tongue leashed. His neighbours too would stand up for her and laugh at him. No, he had no wish to suffer humiliation at this age. He was not a brazen-faced person.

Birij Das came to meet him in the afternoon that day. Iswar was seated on a stool in front of the office. Calling him aside, Birij spoke to him about Kartik.

"Your son's intentions are not good, Iswarda. He is after me to get you declared unfit so that he might have your job. What do you have to say?"

Iswar turned slowly to look at Birij. In his eyes there was an expression that Birij could not read. He stood undecided, not knowing what to say. A moment later, Iswar said, "What will I eat? How will I survive if I give up the job? My daughter-in-law has my son under her thumb. I tell you, Babu, Kartik will turn me out in no time."

Birij nodded his head for he understood Iswar's plight. "Don't worry," he said, "As long as I am here, no harm will come to you. I haven't been able to bring you back to the gang but I haven't washed my hands off the matter yet. I will teach Chhotasahib a lesson at the first opportunity."

Having lost two of his fingers, Iswar served sometimes as a peon and sometimes as a chowkidar. According to the authorities, nothing he ever did was right. At last, one day he summoned all his courage and spoke to the officer, "Sahib, please send me back to my old job. I do not find any comfort here."

"Then why don't you leave?"

Iswar shrank back in fear. Looking at his pale, wrinkled face, Chhotasahib said sympathetically, "You are growing old, Iswar. You need rest. I think I should take you in as my bungalow-peon."

Iswar had always looked down upon the job of a bungalow-peon. He had in store many bitter experiences to narrate. With washing the Memsahib's petticoats and taking the dog out twice a day, the peon had little time left for anything else. So Iswar said 'no' directly.

The officer looked at Iswar intently. The slight twitch of his moustache and the frown on his face spoke of anger. In a stern voice he said to Iswar, "What is it then that you want? A salary without work? You are unfit as a gangman, so you have no other alternatives other than working as a chowkidar."

The job of a chowkidar needed less effort. Still Iswar could not forget his old days, when the work involved hard labour but there was also fun associated with it. When Radhelal, Tiwari, Paswan, Tridib, Maheshwar and the rest of the gang called out to him as they paddled on with the spade and the pick-axe balanced on their shoulders, Iswar sat there wistfully gazing at them in silence. He remembered the days when he too had been a part of that working group and now he so longed to be with them again. Oh! To hear the sound of the pick-axe as it hit the railway lines and the rattle of the stones, and above all, to work a job that satisfied his soul! No one could understand his anguish but it continued to prey upon his mind. Tears flowed down his wizened cheeks and he felt as if, from a distance, the railway tracks were calling him. And the call became one with the voice that rose within him. How could he ignore the call?

Looking at the dirty bicycle that had been his companion for thirty-five long years but lay untouched now, Iswar was filled with nostalgia. As he sat on the charpoy staring at the well-known faces, he could not control himself. What had he not done? Whether it was changing the sleeper or packing chips or cleaning drains, Iswar was always ready. His dedication earned him respect from his colleagues who always held him and his word in high regard. But that was in the past, thought Iswar. Today his condition was like the river that had dried to a trickle, baring the sand ribs.

What pained Iswar the most was that there were many of his age still working on the railway tracks. Ramdhan was still in service. Every morning he went riding his cycle. The aluminium tiffin-carrier in which he carried his mid-day meals hung from the handle.

Iswar could hear Ramdhan's words distinctly. It was as if Ramdhan was standing right beside him, drawing his attention to the trains that went flashing past.

"What speed! What force! A gang of a thousand labourers is nothing compared to it. So many people travel from here to there by train. We are like doctors. When the trains are in trouble, we look after them. The work sounds simple but it needs courage and strength. If you are not bold and strong, then this job is not for you."

A bold Iswar, sincere in his duty, could always do the work of ten single-handedly. He had not learnt the art of hoodwinking; all work was pleasure to him.

The others often asked, "Why do you work so hard, Iswar?" And Iswar had always smiled at such questions. He used to tell them, "Work keeps one fresh and active." Then he asked them, "Can toil and hard work waste one's energy and vitality?"

Others in the gang would listen to him in open-mouthed wonder. Old Iswar was a model to behold and to follow.

Iswar did not seek the shelter of the tree even when the rain came down in torrents. He always said to his co-workers, "If the line is saved, I am saved, my family is saved." Rain or sun, it was all the same to Iswar. With a smile on his lips, he took everything in his stride. In the beginning, Iswar worked at the main down line. It was his duty to ensure that the line was free of obstructions and the trains passed safely. He set out early in the morning every day with a hammer in hand and a red flag folded neatly in his bag. He commanded respect from the tribals as he walked with measured steps, determined to uphold the honour of the Railways and of the uniform that he wore. At times like this, he looked brighter than the trees that glowed in the morning light.

It had been raining in torrents for three days. A huge boulder had come loose and fallen on the railway track right at the point where the line curved sharply. The line was completely blocked. Iswar could not decide on a course of action. The express train was due in a short time. It was impossible now to run back to the station to ask for help. The train moving at high speed would collide with the huge boulder, and then...? An anxious Iswar trembled in fear. Finding no other alternative, Iswar wrapped the red flag around him and stood motionless like a pillar in between the tracks. Tall like the deodar tree, Iswar stood erect with his eyes fixed on the tracks. The express train was approaching. The engine whistled once, a loud and piercing sound. In the glow of the headlamps the driver spotted the living pillar. He pulled the emergency brakes and the snorting, puffing train came to a screeching halt. The driver jumped down and ran to Iswar. There was considerable excitement at the spot. Questions were hurled at Iswar who trembled with fear and excitement. For a full five minutes, he could not speak. The driver, the guard and the passengers wanted to reward Iswar but he refused it humbly.

"Babu, this is my *dipti*, this is where I shine; the Government pays me for this. And that is sufficient for me and my family."

Memories of the yesteryears came rushing back to him in torrents and Iswar cried out, "Stop!" It was too much for him to bear. Sitting there, with no one to share his joys, his sorrows and his memories with, Iswar felt very alone.

Birij often came to chat with Iswar. But strangely, Birij's words failed to comfort him. His grief and sorrow knew no bounds and he said to Birij, "Nobody values my life, babu. The sooner I touch the feet of God, the better. I have no hopes, no desires, nothing to look forward to."

"Don't be silly. Enjoy life with your hard-earned retirement benefits. Spend your days watching your grandchildren grow. It is always a delight to watch children at play. Why worry?"

"Can anybody live without worry?"

"What is the cause of your worry, Iswarda?"

Iswar did not reply immediately. Instead, he looked up at the vast blue expanse and said in a low voice, "Babu, please see to it that I am cremated in the burning ghat that is close to the railway tracks. This is all that I ask for."

"Oh, come on! You will live a long life. Where would we find men like you these days?"

Nothing irritated Kartik and his wife more than listening to such words. Stamping their feet in disgust, they walked away. Poor Iswar! He could only stare at their retreating figures. He had no words to say in protest.

Kartik wanted a job in the Railways. A permanent job. Hawking fruits was too lowly, too menial. It was tiring too. So, very often, he voiced his grievances. Iswar understood everything. Yet how could he give up his job? It wasn't easy even after all these years. It would be easier to pluck out his heart. This thought robbed him of his sleep and he lay awake at night trying to arrive at some solution. An unknown fear tightened its grip upon Iswar. The darkness in the hut was oppressive and after sometime, Iswar felt that he would yield to his son's wishes. The very next moment he changed his mind. What if his son did not look after him anymore? Where would he seek shelter then? Kartik spent his days roaming about with petty thieves. There was always a frown on his face. Iswar felt scared. In the darkness of night, he had seen Kartik moving around the railway tracks. There was something suspicious about it. The old man looked at his son intently, trying to fathom his thoughts. The other day Kartik had given his wife three hundred rupees! In a low voice he had told her to be careful.

"Keep the money and see that the old man knows nothing about it."

"Why? What is the harm if he does?" hissed Phelna in anger. "It's time he left the world. Then you will not have to go out at night."

"Keep quiet. What are you saying?"

"Why will I keep quiet? The man who cannot bear to see his son established in life has no right to live."

Phelna's scathing remarks were extremely agonising. Her manner of talking was what hurt Iswar the most. Still he could not tell her anything. He was too scared of her and her remarks.

In the dark, Iswar cried out like a child in his nightmare. Kartik turned on his side while Phelna said in contempt, "What misery! So many people fall sick, but nothing ever happens to your father!" Iswar lay wide awake after this. He tossed restlessly as he stared into the dark night. Outside, the nightbirds flew in circles, round and round, calling to their mates. The old man spotted a falling star and was overcome by a sense of futility and despair. He felt that he had unknowingly been creating trouble in his son's life. He had deprived them of all the things that made life meaningful and robbed their peace of mind. He felt ashamed of himself and wanted to bid goodbye to his life which now seemed to be a burden to him. But in the end he resisted the urge to commit suicide. He was too much in love with himself. No, he could not take away the life that God had given him. Why should he try to commit suicide on these railway tracks which had given him a sense of fulfillment in the past? How could he, the man who cleared the chips, now cover them with his own red blood? He went back to his hut.

In the afternoon, there was a quarrel again. Kartik had gone out with his cart. On his return, he vented his anger upon his old father. Iswar had just sat down to eat a mouthful of rice when he heard Kartik's rude, accusing words, "You don't want to see me happy. You don't lend a helping hand in the daily chores. My wife is pregnant, yet she has to slog. If you could at least carry a bucketful of water, it would be of immense help to her." Iswar looked on in amazement. Phelna sat nearby, sulking. Then, with an angry expression on her face she said, "As if he is the only man going out on night duty."

Iswar was still silent, unprotesting. And what could he say to those who refused to listen to reason?

As per the instruction of Chhotasahib, Iswar had been appointed as the store chowkidar. There was no chance of going back to the gang. So he tried his best to forget the past and carry on as a chowkidar. There was no other way out.

Iswar stayed awake the whole night; he would never shirk his responsibility. Just a few days back he had caught the truck that was trying to smuggle out chips and gravel. Sensing danger, the driver had tried to bribe Iswar. But no. His shouts and words of protest drew in the people of the railway colony. They tied up the driver while Iswar spoke over the telephone to Chhotasahib regarding the turn of events. With sleepy eyes Sahib arrived, but instead of praising Iswar for his brave deed, Chhotasahib rebuked him, much to his shame and consternation.

"What have you done? Just set him free. Who asked you to be so bold? Such disturbing elements!"

Poor Iswar! With dismay he had asked Sahib, "Should I then worship him?"

"Shut up! Just do as I say, else there will be trouble in store for you. Go, untie the knots. Remember, you are an unfit gangman, not a policeman," Sahib said cruelly.

Iswar did as he was asked. This was the first shock that he received. That day he tried to reason with himself.

"Perhaps there is no God after all. That is why my good deeds bring me such humiliation."

The matter did not end there. The senior officer came to know about it. He rebuked his junior, Chhotasahib, in the presence of all the staff. Beaming with pride, he clapped Iswar on his shoulders.

"Well done, Iswar. Carry on with your work. If you face any difficulty, contact me directly. I have been informed about your sincerity. When the time comes, I will surely recommend your name for the General Manager's Award."

Since that day, Iswar had had no regrets. Birij said to him enthusiastically, "Didn't I tell you often that there are good people? This is the time. Sahib is pleased with you and your selfless service. Now you can speak to him about Kartik's job. I am sure he will not disappoint you."

Iswar had been thinking of Birij's words while on his way to his post of duty that night. For the past few days, he had been feeling sad though he did not quite know why. He found it difficult to work like he used to before. Kartik's future troubled him. Before retirement he would find some job for Kartik in the Railways. Or else how would he face his future?

It was a ten-minute walk to the store from his hut. In the darkness the tracks shone like sharp swords. Iswar had a three-battery torch with him and a bamboo stick. He needed these things for guarding the store. The stick, of course, was not only for safety. It was a support for his old limbs. He often stumbled as he walked on the uneven roads. The stick helped him to stand straight like Kartik.

Unlike earlier, Phelna did not hand him the torch. Iswar brought it down from the rooftop himself. Not only this, she hardly spoke. Even Kartik seemed more serious. With innumerable tears Phelna had told Kartik about his father's ill ways,"Your father's character is not good. When I was changing my saree, he kept on staring at me. I beg of you, please drop me at my father's home. I don't want to stay here with him staring at me. One day I will be utterly ruined."

Kartik knew that his wife was not speaking the truth. Yet he remained silent. He had become accustomed to the comfort that money bought. It would do no good to irritate his father. All their show-off depended upon his father's earning. Although he was scared of his wife, at that moment, her disparaging words failed to create any impact on Kartik who was lost in thought. That night was going to determine his future.

After walking a few steps, Iswar stopped. He caught the stick firmly and sighed, "Oh God, forgive them. And if my eyes have sinned, then pluck them out. Make me blind once and for all."

Then Iswar burst out crying. In the darkness of the night the heart-rending sobs of the old man filled the air. The church clock announced the time. Iswar wiped his eyes and stood up. As he went past the level-crossing gate carefully, he looked up to see the starlit sky and the crescent moon.

Iswar sat silently. He was not habituated to working the night shift, yet he remained awake. The sleepers were piled up in one corner, the gravel in the other. The whole area was littered with iron rods. Iswar looked at it intently. Sometimes he walked around. If on this dark, silent night Iswar fell asleep, nobody would question him. But Iswar had brought only a bedsheet with him. When the mosquitoes attacked in large numbers, Iswar wrapped himself in it. If he felt drowsy, he washed his eyes and then stared at the materials scattered all over the yard. The rails began to hum. He heard the shrill whistle of the engine and watched the train hiss past him. The trains ran with no consideration for the clock. The rhythmic beat of the wheels, the light from the compartments and the shrill whistles shattered the silence of the night for only a little while. Then peace was restored. The dogs barked in the dark.

Iswar sat guarding the store, unafraid of the darkness. He lit a *bidi* to keep himself alert.

At one-thirty the mail train passed and the bats on the branches of the arjun tree flew away. On any other day Iswar would have kept watch on their movement. But today he was too tired. He rested against the neem tree and looked in wonder at its bright green leaves. By and by, a sweet fragrance reached his nostrils and made him drowsy. Covering himself with the bedsheet, Iswar lay down on the green grass. The sweet fragrance of the neem flowers wiped away the musty smell from his body. The neem flowers laid out a bed for him.

In his dream the exhausted, upset and confused Iswar saw Chhotasahib, Kartik and Phelna. In ugly contrast against the backdrop of soothing nature stood his employer, his son and his daughter-in-law, revealing their true colours that had so long been hidden from view. Old Iswar shuddered to see the group of three degenerates, dehumanised by their greed.

Birij Das appeared covered with sweat. Placing a hand on Iswar's forehead he told him to sleep. They were awake, he reassured him; Iswar had nothing to worry about.

But Iswar could not sleep. Just a few paces from him, the pile of sleepers suddenly crashed. With sleepy eyes, Iswar could spot a truck loaded with sleepers. Before he could rush out, some seven men climbed up onto the moving truck as it sped away into the night.

Only one in the group could not and he ran after the truck, desperate to get to safety. Iswar followed and very soon he caught up with the man. As he flashed the torchlight, his grip loosened and a cry came out from the very depths of his being.

"Keto, you!"

Before he could complete the sentence, Kartik, whom his father lovingly called Keto, turned around. His eyes betrayed a horrifying and brutal fear. He sprang upon his father. His sinewy, muscular hands tightened around his father's throat in a vice-like grip. Iswar felt terrible pain as he gasped for breath. In a raspy voice, he tried to tell his son how wrong he was. Then darkness closed in on him. Before leaving, Kartik placed Iswar's body on the railway tracks. The whole night Iswar lay there. The moon and the stars kept watch on him, the neem flowers fell gently upon his breast as though they were paying their last respects to the simple, unassuming god, Iswar.

The veil of glimmering twilight withdrew. The dawn, pure and fresh, began to reveal itself. The eastern sky glowed bright red and touched Iswar's face in a last caress. The passing gang-men stopped short in their tracks lamenting the loss of their Iswardada who was now only a spectre, the last remains of poor humanity after a lifelong and sad struggle.

Kartik and Phelna rushed to the spot in the morning. They seemed to faint every now and then. Birij Das tried to console them. The senior officer reached the scene having received the message over telephone. So did Chhotasahib. In a sad voice he said, "This is so unfortunate. The man was mentally unbalanced." A feeble protest could be heard from Birij but it was quickly brushed aside, for Kartik supported Chhotasahib, "Sahib is right, Babu. My father had lost his mental balance. His untimely death will ruin us."

As per Iswar's last wish, he was cremated in the burning ghat by the railway line, using the unused railway sleepers for wood. Only ten sleepers were enough to reduce the body of Iswar, the gangman, to ashes.

Kartik returned home after the cremation. Having stood face-to-face with death, he was suddenly aware of his own mortality. Looking solemnly at Phelna, he said in a tearful voice, "Phelna, dear, the shade has now retreated. The man whom I cremated today was a very good man. See, there is no smoke from his pyre. What if one day your flesh and blood too kills me in the same manner?"

Translated by Anuradha Sen

THE LEPER

Winter nights were a torture to the old and aged. Wrapping his torn and worn-out shawl around him, Dasarath sat huddled on his bed. Silver moonlight flooded the landscape. A fierce cold wind blew around the poor hut. The silence of the night was occasionally broken by the shrill bark of a pariah dog.

Dasarath tried to sleep. But unable to, he sat up—it was the fourth time he had done so. There was still no sign of Bhogi. Before leaving, Bhogi had grinned at him toothily and said, "Don't you worry, Uncle. I'll just go and come back before you can even call my name."

That was early in the morning. Darkness was setting in and Bhogi was yet to return. The cold, biting wind had driven everybody indoors. The roads were empty. Sometimes Dasarath could hear bits of conversation among people returning from the feast. Nobody came by this side of the village. During daytime, this area had the stillness of a burning ghat: silent, mysterious, and fearful. At night there was cold darkness.

All waiting ends at some point. It has to end. Dasarath knew this but his wait seemed to be never-ending. Bhogi was to bring him rice and mutton. Dasarath longed to satisfy his hunger with it and then sleep a sound sleep. Afternoon passed. The evening gave way to night but there was no sign of Bhogi. He was nowhere in sight. Dasarath did not want to cook for himself. It was a lot of trouble. The smoke from the firewood and the heat of the fire made his eyes burn. He was bent double with age and poverty, and his waist protested in pain every time he sat on his haunches. The pus and the sores were no less painful. Pain and hunger had a hundred mouths—which mouth would he feed?

Every morning Kanai Siuli passed by his house. Close by and a little away from the main road, he had set up his workplace. He had huge stoves and all day long he boiled the sap and juice of date palm. As their eyes met, Kanai came up and gave Dasarath a pot full of juice. Holding the brass pot that contained about a seer of juice, Dasarath became unmindful. He dreamt, of a hundred date palms with hundreds of earthen pots tied to them—not a drop was to be wasted. Kanai's father Jagai sat boiling the juice. With leaves of date palm in his hand, Jagai sat watchful and alert, making sure that not a single bubble fell on the ground. It was a tough job yet Jagai sat there, thrashing the rising bubbles in the big vessels with the leaves.

Dasarath sighed. It seemed so long ago in the past but it was just a few years back. Jagai did not come anymore, he could no longer walk, he stumbled and fell often. Dasarath himself felt so old, so miserably old. Because of his old-sightedness, he could not see clearly. There were wrinkles all over his body and he walked very slowly. He was always tired and had breathing problems too.

People think leprosy is a dirty disease. The leper soon becomes an outcast through no fault of his. Dasarath wondered why it was him who had to be afflicted by this much-dreaded disease. Whose curse was it that brought it upon him? This thought haunted him day and night. His head reeled if he thought for long and he felt drowsy. But even in sleep he had no respite. The blood-red eyes of the disease kept threatening him. Poor Dasarath cried out in fear. There was nothing he could do.

Nothing except waiting. Waiting for the curtain to drop, for his uneventful life to end, waiting to walk into the abode of Yama, the God of Death.

The sores that had covered most of his body smelled bad. The disease left his nails damaged and crooked like the *sukni* fish. His feet were in no better condition. The sores and the cracks were so painful that Dasarath had to tie thick bandage all over. This stopped his skin from rubbing against something rough. He was thin and gaunt with deep wrinkles in his skin.

Ramchandra, his only son, got married just two days ago; they were celebrating with great pomp. Dasarath heard about it but his son did not care to inform him. The villagers had tried to reason with Ram. "After all, he is your father. Meet him at least once. Seek his blessings. Whatever it is, he is your father. You should not forget him." But Ramchandra, Dasarath's only son and the chief of the village, did not care to listen. He had screamed furiously, "I will not go! He is not my father! He is my staunch enemy. It is for him that I have to suffer. Everybody looks down upon me. Not one but ten marriage negotiations have failed. All because of him, my father!" He paused and then continued, "This is the eleventh one. I cannot go to my father and ruin this one too." Ram's eyes betrayed pain and fear. He said, "Consider that I don't have a father. I have nobody."

This was a shock to Dasarath. He had never imagined such betrayal. At night his heart cried out for his son. He had brought up Ram with such love and care. When he joined high school, Dasarath had bought a cycle for him. He didn't have the heart to say 'no' to his son's childish demand for a cycle. How many in the village had a cycle in those days? Again, when Ram had wanted a radio, Dasarath did not think twice. His wife Sarada had told him repeatedly not to indulge him so much. But Dasarath had paid no heed to her words. He had sold the jute at a throwaway price to buy his son a radio. Now the same son looked down upon him, even though this behaviour harmed the reputation of the family. Sarada was right, thought Dasarath sadly. She always said, "Such pampering is not good. One day he will trample all over your feelings. He will be beyond all control." A dejected Dasarath remembered how he had rebuked his wife then. "Keep quiet, woman. Don't speak ill." Today he realised the truth in Sarada's words. Ram had not only run away breaking the chains of love, but also smeared his father's face with disgrace.

Today, however, Dasarath could not control himself. It was a day to rejoice. It was the *boubhat*. The ceremony would be followed by a grand feast. And here Dasarath was all alone.

Bhogi had said he would bring rice and mutton for Dasarath. That kept him awake for so long. *It is quite late,* thought Dasarath, though he had no means of knowing the time. As an old and frail leper, he possessed a strong will and let pure emotion guide him. A cold draught played about in the room. Sometimes the call of the nightbird could be heard and sometimes the cicada. But these sounds were rare and quickly swallowed up by the silence. When the dog heard the strange sounds, it ran out from the verandah, barking.

Dasarath stared at the lantern. He felt so old, so miserably old. His jaws pained every time he tried to breathe. In his toothless mouth, only the gum remained like a narrow ridge of earth around a waterbody. Whenever he spoke loudly, he spattered saliva. His mouth tasted bitter. "It's the juice. I should not have had it," thought Dasarath. He felt nauseous and the bilious belch made him feel weak. It would have been good if Bhogi was around. He could have fetched water and called the doctor. Finally, after having cleared his bowels, he felt relieved.

In the morning he had asked Bhogi if he could attend the ceremony. Bhogi remained quiet. He scratched the floor of the verandah with his toes.

"Ram will surely come here at least once."

"Dada is very busy. He has no time."

"Your aunt?"

"Aunt is busy too. Don't you understand? It's her son's marriage. She has the keys to the house, the store, everything. Who knows what will be needed when!"

"Oh!" sighed Dasarath. His eyes filled with tears, "Let them not come. I have done my duty. I have followed the teachings of my religion—God is my judge."

Bhogi did not wait any longer. Who liked to listen to such philosophical talk? Nobody needs old oxen to plough the land. The lonely Dasarath too did not wait. He went directly to the garden—his garden that he had planted and looked after. The marigold plants, the densely growing spinach, the fence of bamboo—every single thing that grew here knew the touch of his hands. Just in front of the verandah was the platform for the tulsi plant. He watered it every day after his bath.

Jagai was fortunate. His eldest son took him to the shed where he worked. He fed his father parched rice and molasses. Dasarath sighed. It was not any ordinary sap, it was nectar. Bad times begin for a father when his son grows up. Ramchandra was the village chief. He worked for the welfare of the villagers, but he had no time for his father. He did not even care to know whether his father was dead or alive. When his own son had no time for him, what claim could he possibly have on Bhogi? He was an orphan who stayed with him for a square meal. What did he understand of life and its complexities?

Old Jagai had come to meet Dasarath. Jagai could not stand straight and he always had a walking stick with him. Yet, he came. He, his son Kanai, and Bhogi were the only ones who came here. Others were too scared. Nobody ever made the mistake of coming here. It was as if Yama would catch them straight. Leprosy would spread all over their bodies.

People from all the neighbouring villages were invited, yet Dasarath had not been asked. In the afternoon he had some rice with only onion and chilli. He knew that meanwhile preparations for the ceremony were on in full swing. Jagai, looking at Dasarath, had said in jest that it was *his* day, the day of his son's marriage.

Dasarath looked long and fixedly at Jagai. He could not say anything in reply. Indeed, it was his son's marriage, but his son did not acknowledge him. His eldest daughter had come to attend the wedding, but even she was stopped. All of this was Ram's policy. With whom could Dasarath speak about such matters?

Jagai sat down, made himself comfortable and said, "I was not doing too well. Whooping cough. So Kanai went to Basantpur. He met the ayurvedic physician there. The medicine has helped, so I feel much better now."

"Basantpur! So far! Kanai went there?"

"Why won't he? After all, I am his father. He is illiterate but he cares for me. Here, see, he got me this shawl. He bought it with the money he got by selling jaggery. Fifty rupees it cost! See, feel it. Well, when will the bullock cart come for you?"

"I am not going."

"Why? How can you say so? If you are not present there, how can Ram marry?"

Dasarath had spent quite a few nights hoping, waiting for the bullock cart that never came. The bridegroom and the rest of his party went by the reserved bus. Dasarath stood there like a statue. His eyes were red—was it the dust?

Bhogi, outspoken as always, had said, "You are crying, Uncle?"

"No. Why should I cry?" Dasarath tried to wipe away the tears and laughed. The twelve-year-old Bhogi had understood on that fateful day that even laughter can be painful and soul-searing. He had tried to comfort Dasarath like a wise man, "I have no one, Uncle. Let all this get over, then I will take you to the hospital."

"I will not go anywhere. Not anymore."

"That is not right." Bhogi spoke like a doctor and said, "Why are you scared of a disease? Weren't you a freedom fighter?

You had been a part of the struggle; you had been imprisoned. Breaking down in the face of such small matters is not befitting of you."

"I am not scared of the disease. I am scared of the people and their attitude. I cannot endure it anymore."

"I understand."

"Do you know there was no hospital in this village? People would die without treatment. We had sent so many petitions and only then this hospital was built. Dr Bidhan Chandra Roy was the Chief Minister then. That year, he visited our village for the first time. How do I tell you about those days? What a great and noble man he was! He treated me with respect. And today my own son hates me."

Reminiscing of the doctor's words filled old Dasarath with hope and determination. He wanted to live and to enjoy life once again. The words were like the cool breeze that offered solace to his bruised heart. His son Ram was literate but he had failed as a human being. He had not given his father even a quarter of the respect that the CM had. Is not such behaviour heart-rending? Previously, his meals would come from Ram's house. Sarada too would come occasionally and enquire about this and that. She no longer came these days. Actually, she was too scared of Ram. She always cowered before him.

Just two years after Ramchandra became the village chief, he acquired about two acres of land and a motorcycle. He went from village to village exchanging greetings, talking to people and sharing their joys and sorrows. Standing against Ram in the elections was Sadananda, a local leader who belonged to the opposition party. In the meetings held at the local weekly market, he had tried to make the villagers see the simple truth: how could they believe that the chief would work for their betterment? "The man who does not look after his own aged father, will he look after you? Yes, he can read and write, but that is not enough."

On hearing such taunting remarks, Ramchandra had taken his father to the hospital. He had arranged for a check-up and medicines. Finally, when they had returned home late in the evening, Ram had threatened his father.

"I don't want to see that Sadananda fellow at your home. Do you understand? If I see him there, there will be bloodshed. He belongs to the opposition party. He is trying to make this an issue to win the election."

Dasarath had questioned Ram about the elections. Ram said, "All lies! Who told you all this? I'm sure it was that rascal Sadananda. If I have stolen public money, then why would the people vote for me? Do you think people are blind?"

These words disturbed Dasarath. He could not sleep; he was restless, he could feel a pain in his chest. He realised that disease was slowly spreading all over the village. It was in the breeze, in the dust, in the flowers and fruits; it was everywhere. The entire village seemed to be mourning in a deep black darkness.

Dasarath turned over in fear. A cold winter fog slowly enveloped the village barely lit by the dim light of the moon. There were no sounds except for loud laments carried by the wind. And the noise of dogs fighting over leftovers. He felt terribly hungry. How long could he endure it? He bent low to take out some puffed rice kept under his bed and started chewing it. His hope had increased his hunger. He had longed to eat to his heart's content at his son's wedding. Was it so much to hope for? But God could not grant him even this. Ramchandra was a big man. A busy man. But what about Sarada? Couldn't she come once at least? If she wished, she surely could have. Dasarath knew why Sarada did not come. But where had Bhogi vanished? He had promised to return early: "Uncle, I will go and be back before you know it. I will watch the fireworks and come back. I don't like to stay there. They only tell me to clear the scraps and leftovers." *Why do you go then? Is there any shortage of working hands there?* Dasarath thought.

Earlier, Dasarath had looked at Bhogi carefully and said, "You have eaten a lot, haven't you? Surely you had mutton?"

"Oh yes. After all it is dada's marriage."

"All of you ate such delicious food. Everyone except me."

"Why will be you left out? I will bring it for you. Have patience. Let the darkness set in, then..."

No matter how hard Bhogi tried to bring Dasarath rice and mutton, Ram would not allow him. He had to eat only vegetables. It must be about two years since he last tasted meat. Ramchandra had spread word that Dasarath should not eat it. The doctors however had told him that there was no need for a restricted diet.

Bhogi sometimes brought him fish on the sly, that was all. It was a dream to eat rice and mutton. Two birds came and danced near the bamboo fence every evening. Dasarath had tried to kill the two but couldn't. Even Bhogi had tried. He had information that Ram had mutton every week; he couldn't live only on vegetables. The best fish was always reserved for Ram. Having earned a little money, Ram did as he pleased.

Bhogi said, "The bride is so beautiful. She has big eyes and an oval face. When she smiles, it is a full smile. And how well she speaks! You never feel like turning away."

"Will you take me there once?" Dasarath asked eagerly, his eyes full of appeal. "I would dearly like to see the Lakshmi of the house. Who knows when I might die, and this wish remain unfulfilled."

"How can I? Dada will not send her here. But we can do one thing."

"What?"

"She goes to the pond in the afternoon. Exactly at twelve when the minibus leaves. Hide behind the bushes. No one will know."

"Don't be stupid."

"There is no other way."

"I am not going to hide to see my own daughter-in-law. Then I will have truly lost everything. I only want to see her face. Will I be chopped into pieces for this?"

Dasarath sat there gloomily. The puffed rice was stuck in his dry throat, so he drank a little water. He hated himself. Didn't people fall sick? But to suffer like this was too much. He had not committed any wrongs willfully. Then why this trial? Looking at his shrunk fingers, Dasarath wished he were no longer alive. His hands looked frightful: nails were missing and the bones were visible. Would he lose all ten fingers in his lifetime? All of the body is lost eventually, but one sets out on his eternal journey before that happens. What was the use of trying to hold on to the bent and broken cage? Dasarath pressed his fingers hard. The red flesh stared back at him. His fingers pained. His toes looked hideous. His legs had shrunk. It hurt if he tried to walk fast. If he stumbled and fell, they started bleeding. At night Dasarath was scared to lie down. If his skin rubbed against the shawl, blood oozed out and the foul smell of the sores filled the room. It was difficult to change the bandage. Pieces of thread nearly always remained stuck in the soft flesh of the wounds. Any sort of pull caused bleeding. Even ointment could not cure the sores on his heels. Dust and sand irritated his skin.

On this lonely night, Dasarath lay calmly, listening to the music of the shehnai. Many a question came to his mind and disturbed his peace. Was he Ramchandra's father or the chief's servant?

"It wasn't right of Ramchandra, you know," Jagai had told him.

These words failed to comfort Dasarath. He said, "He is not my son, he's a serpent. I should have killed him the very moment he was born. He has the audacity to tell me that leprosy is an infectious disease, and so I should live alone in one isolated corner of the village."

"Didn't his mother say anything?"

"What will she say? She only cried. Then she came and left me here. My eldest daughter used to visit me. But I suppose my son and son-in-law have stopped her."

Dasarath could not sleep at night. He stared at the main road, though nothing could be clearly seen. Sometimes bits of conversation reached him.

"It's been ages since I tasted such yoghurt."

"What about the mutton? Oh, what taste!"

"You know where the cook has come from? All the way from Berhampore!"

There was no end to the excitement; people speculated about the number of invitees and discussed how many people it would take to devour all the mutton in those huge containers. Lavish arrangements had been made. One could eat as much as they wanted. There was no parsimony. Elections, of course, were knocking at the door.

Dasarath looked at the earthen pot. There was still some rice left in it. In winter, the rice didn't go bad as easily. If he wished to, he could have eaten it. In fact, he would have done that any other day. But not today. Today his eyes looked out for Bhogi who would return with rice and mutton. Dasarath wanted to call out, "Ei Bhogi, Bhogii…" But he couldn't.

The dog was his only companion. It was strong and well-built. It lay comfortably on the verandah looking at Dasarath all the while.

Dasarath took his walking stick and straightened himself as much as he could. His body cried out in pain, the sores protested, yet he walked down the steps. His waist was unable to support the weight of his body which was thus bent low like a young shoot of bamboo. His old, bearded face was tinged with sorrow. The wrinkles on his face spoke of years of experience. The deep scar on his forehead was a gift from the British police—a mark of the freedom struggle. His broad forehead had endured the attacks bravely. There was a vast difference between yesterday's generation and today's. He had never taken any bribe or asked for a favour, never tricked or fooled anybody. Yet he had leprosy. Why? For which sin? For the sins of his past life or the present one?

Dasarath started walking slowly. He was no longer hungry. He wasn't sad either. It was not possible to have every desire fulfilled. This was destined to be. Nobody had the power to remould their life according to their wishes. He had no financial trouble. His pension was enough. He didn't have to beg. He had everything, yet somehow his sorrow always pricked him like a sharp needle. Life is short. You only live once; there is no second chance.

Dasarath forgot his hunger. He only remembered a beautiful face with a vermillion bindi on her forehead. She sat wearing a Banarasi saree while the music of the shehnai floated across the village. To Dasarath, the tune was like a beloved beckoning him. Like an inebriated man Dasarath said, "I'll go. Let's see who can stop me."

Dasarath left the main road and walked along the broken path across the field. The moon did not shine brightly in the December sky, but there were innumerable stars and fireflies. There was no fear of snakes since it was winter. He stopped suddenly as a wonderful perfume reached him.

It was on such a night that he and his wife had slept on a bed of flowers prepared by his sisters-in-law and the curious neighbours. Sarada was a young girl then, shy and nervous. Adorned with jewellery and flowers, his wife had walked in with nervous steps. She was wearing a red saree and her shyness made her blush. She looked so beautiful. This reminiscence gave Dasarath a sudden bout of happiness that filled him with new strength and energy. Wrapping the shawl tightly around himself, he listened to what the passersby had to say.

"Beautiful bride."

"The chief is lucky."

"Yes. A real goddess."

Blood rose in his old veins and he shivered. What if he was chased away from there? He stopped and pondered for a moment and then, because he had not learnt to accept failure, he began walking again. He would not be an obstacle in their happiness and merrymaking. The backyard would surely be open to him even if the main entrance was not.

Somebody ran towards the temple with a lantern. A few young boys stood smoking, cautiously avoiding the shops and the temple. Dasarath came and stood just behind Ram's house. He could see clearly in the light which reached him. The thought of the delicious meal made him restless. He could not decide what to do next. It was not safe to stand there. Anybody could see him and then there would be trouble.

The sounds of music and laughter and bits of conversation held no meaning for Dasarath. He walked on carefully till a piece of broken glass made him sit down. The pain was too much. His face twisted in an effort to keep silent. Dasarath pulled out the piece of glass from his foot and limped towards the new building. He was able to ignore the physical pain and concentrated on the task at hand. Right in front of the two buildings stood a proud peacock. A wonderful piece of art. There was a fence all around it. He walked slowly. Bhogi had told him that Ram's wife was in the new building. He had no other concern. He stopped. Then the next moment, he saw his son, happy and proud, speaking to his guests.

If he kept standing there and watching, the whole night would soon pass. He moved close to the compost heap. Somebody was relieving himself there. Dasarath covered his nose and took two steps backward. It was difficult not to be seen in such places. Would he be able to cross the heap of manure? He did not have enough strength left in him to jump across it. All the scraps from the feast had been dumped there on the heap. One could smell the ghee just as strongly as the cow dung. There were dogs roaming about.

Dasarath climbed down carefully. There was the chance he might slip and fall. One uncalculated step would betray his presence. He lifted his dhoti so that it would not be soiled. He was close to his destination when somebody dropped a basketful of leftovers and scraps all over him in the darkness.

Dasarath swayed and then fell straight into the heap. The hungry dogs came running and jumped onto the heap in search of food.

In a moment began the fight for survival between the man and the dogs. The lone wail of the man slowly stifled the notes of the shehnai.

Translated by Anuradha Sen

THE PALANQUIN

The Parijan was headed towards Daudpur. Beyond the village of Nankha lay a vast field, barren and craggy. Throughout the dry summer, hot winds blew over the region. The narrow path along the side of the weaver's house went right up to the field of Danga-Pariya. There were knee-high ridges in the ground in this section of the field. All over the ground, there were distinct marks left by the wheels of bullock-carts. The winding path went this way and that; it slithered like a serpent under the hedge, the thorny bushes, and the broken huts to meet the Panchayati dam. Close to the broken path stood a cluster of date palms, broken and bent having been struck by lightning. On the high bank was the ancient burning-ghat. It was across this area and along this road that the Parijan went. It was bound for Muralimohanbabu's house.

The six bearers hurried. They had covered many miles at a brisk pace, yet there was no time to stop. Very soon the heatwaves would make it difficult for them to travel. Already their eyes were blinded by the burning hot sun. The others had gone ahead. The men had loads fastened to the ends of the long poles balanced on their shoulders. The palanquin carried the bridegroom's maternal uncle and a rohu fish that weighed exactly twenty kilos as well as a trunk with all the finery for the bride.

There was a fireworks display. A young fellow from the bridegroom's side hung a *dodoma* on the tree and lit the match. The sound was deafening. The next moment, a rocket darted through the air. The sound could be heard far and wide. People came running to see the show. They came out curious and amazed, and stayed to rejoice and make merry. The young girls and the young wives faced the most trouble trying to keep their sarees in place as the strong wind sent the loose ends of their sarees flying. Their feet were lined with *alta*. The children came hopping and skipping from school with eyes wide open in wonder. They cried out in pain as the sharp cracks in the ground lacerated their feet.

The Parijan had not been seen in the village in a long time. The village had neither the occasion nor the means. There were no crops. The water level had receded to the bowels of the earth. The fields looked ugly; the farmers had no work. Lush green fields and a rich harvest were things of the remote past. Even the landowners had no peace. The land was parched and cracked. Water and manure no longer brought in profit. And where there was no gain, Lakshmi, the Goddess of Wealth, did not appear. So the village had nearly forgotten the Parijan.

Fireworks had last been displayed after the elections. The occasion was the triumphal procession. There was rejoicing in the neighbouring villages. The villagers were dazzled. But all that was a thing of the past. There was no new flavour, no new taste of joy in the village in recent times.

Moina came hurriedly from near the Hari temple. She had gone there to collect dry leaves. This was a daily chore. She was too poor to buy firewood. Even if she wanted to boil just some rice, she needed at least a basketful of dry leaves. She was not allowed to enter the bamboo grove anymore. Bamboo leaves brought forth heat and fire easily, much more easily than the fire in Moina's body. She carried her three-year-old son Bishu with her. He was very thin, nothing but skin and bones, and always hungry. Moina ran. Her saree disorderly, her hair dishevelled, She had beads of sweat all over her forehead; yet she ran.

It was not that she had never seen a palanquin. When she was at Contai with her in-laws, she had gone to Darua for a medical check-up with her husband once. It was there at the bus stand that she had seen a palanquin. As she came half-running, half-walking, memories of the past flashed through her mind, forming a confused lump of nostalgia. Her son was crying for milk. She slapped him hard; still he wouldn't stop crying.

"Can't you die, you pest!" she cursed, her words almost a groan. Feeling the insistent pull at her teat, and left with no option, she stopped under the shade of a tree to give suck to Bishu. He suckled hungrily. Poor boy. What was his fault? He could only rely on his mother's milk when hungry. People passed by continuously. She could hear their excited talk.

"Whose palanquin is it?"

"Look at the decorations! They do have taste."

"Yes, yes."

The six bearers supporting the palanquin on their shoulders by the long sticks heard the excited conversation. The tall one right at the front had red, bloodshot eyes and a hairy chest. Looking directly at Moina, he smiled and made gestures. Moina's face twisted in disgust. Everybody looked at her with eyes full of lust. It was as though she had no roots holding her to the soil, no anchor; whoever got her first would take her. Misfortune never came alone. Otherwise why would her gentle, soft-spoken husband chase her out? Was it her fault that her father could not give the five hundred rupees he had promised to give? Before her father could beg and borrow so that he might keep his word, the raging fire reduced his body to ashes and thus ended her marriage. She came back to her native village. Her father had no landed property. He had left behind a small hut and grinding poverty. But that piece of land and the ancestral hut was not enough to fill her belly. Moina started working. Everybody waited for an opportunity to deceive her. To top it all, her full mouth and her firm, sensuous body made onlookers clench their fists in desire. Her body was a burden to her, a source of anxiety and tension. Moina sent so many letters but her husband never came. He had no reason to come. He had married again. The bride's father was quite well-to-do. He had given his son-in-law a cycle, a wrist watch, a gold finger ring and one thousand rupees in cash. Moina looked at Bishu and trembled in fear. Why she felt afraid she did not know. Beads of sweat appeared on her forehead and she had a distant look in her eyes. At such moments she wanted to curse her father: why didn't he kill her before he died? She was sick of struggling with poverty and its ugliness and meanness.

The six bearers were smoking. Their facial expressions changed every time they drew in smoke. Moina ground her teeth in disgust and got up to go.

Attracted by the sound of an aircraft, her son was looking up towards the sky. The times were not good, the village chief had said. War was imminent.

The romping wind blew in and out of the folds of her saree, exposing her fleshy thigh. Moina tried to gather the folds closer to cover herself. The chief looked at her and said, "Oh, poor girl! There's no end to her troubles. Where will she go? She is still so young."

"There are so many places to go," commented Kanu from the crowd. His father Suren Jana owned the palanquin. He had bought it from Muchiya's father who fell victim to Jana's sly turn of phrase. As a result, Jana got it rather cheap. It was when Muchiya had fallen very sick. A continuous pain in his stomach had taken a toll on his energy and strength. Some said it was a boil, others said it could be ulcer. He had to undergo an operation for which he needed about six to seven thousand rupees. The doctors at the government hospital had prescribed medicines and injections without which Muchiya would not survive. His old father had gone from door to door in vain. Then Suren Jana had lent him one hundred rupees at an interest of fifteen rupees per month. It was on this condition that Muchiya's father had mortgaged the Parijan. Days and months passed. After a year, Muchiya came back with a scar as long as a hand measured from the tip of the thumb to the tip of the little finger. But the palanquin did not return.

Kanu's words filled Moina with anger. The other day, Kanu had tried to take her towards the canal, showing her a twenty-rupee note. Moina had hissed at him, "For shame! Just because you have money, you think you can do whatever you want?" Seeing her here now, Kanu again came near Moina, looking at her with contempt. He would not be thwarted so easily. Taking advantage of the crowd, he touched her once. And then again.

Moina left the place. She could not stand there any longer. She went and stood on the bank, looking pale and listless. She had no one to blame except her fate. Not every girl is fortunate enough to enjoy a conjugal life. At times she even wished for Bishu's death. Her body lost neither its lustre nor its physical appeal even though she passed her days in poverty. A knock on the door on a dark night filled her with fear. She sat huddled with the pestle in her hand. She knew that the door would open wide if anybody pushed it with their leg. She did not know why she could never make people understand that they could not drag her down to their level. These days Muchiya did not speak to her properly. Ever since the palanquin moved to Jana's verandah, Muchiya was out of work and free as a floating balloon. He could not work as a field hand. If he tried to carry a basket full of clay on his head, his stomach protested; a pain started near his navel and he felt nauseous. The other day he came back from Erenda in the evening with great difficulty. He had lain down in the verandah tossing in pain. Initially, Moina did not go to him. She thought she would stay away but finally she had to come. The massage with mustard oil and water had no effect, the pain did not lessen. Finally, she had brought silt from the river and smeared Muchiya's stomach with it. The cold silt had helped. But Moina had to undergo great trouble as her saree had got wet.

Kanu had disappeared. Moina did not wish to see the Parijan anymore. The people surrounded the palanquin. They were engrossed with it. Moina wanted to take this opportunity to run to safety. But tears blinded her vision. She slowed down. She thought of the day when as a newly married bride she had set out with her husband. In the palanquin the husband and wife sat face-to-face. The rains had set in early that year. The fields were all different shades of green. Looking at them, Moina had been overcome with sorrow. How would she live without all these? Her husband had tried to reason with her, "Don't cry, silly girl. Does anyone cry while going to her father-in-law's house? Come on, wipe your tears." Moina had looked up to see a gentle, caring face, with eyes full of love and understanding. The palanquin had stopped on the main road. Friends and relatives had gathered near the palanquin, looking at her with smiling faces. Her old father had wiped his tears and said to her, "Don't worry about me. Obey your father-in-law and mother-in-law. I will be fine."

Tears flowed down her cheeks but she kept on walking. After some time, she met Jhampri and Haguri. They had come with a wicker basket in search of any kind of edible greens. They looked like dolls, dressed in bright yellow sarees with red borders. These summer days there was a scarcity of edible greens too.

These are hard times, Moina thought. People ate vegetables and greens that were normally not eaten. What else could they do? There was no cultivation. First there was drought, then floods. The arid fields looked like a barren woman. On the other side of the canal, people ploughed and tilled the land, but the produce was beyond the reach of the average. Haguri's father went begging from one village to another. He was also a shaman who could chant incantations and bring relief to the sick and the ailing. In summer, people normally remained fit. So did the animals. That is why the old man had no income. He went from door to door and returned with whatever he got. They would eat leftover rice kept steeped in water, along with the edible greens that his daughters gathered. "Haguri, go see the Parijan. Go, go."

Moina had not seen the Parijan carefully. She could not, even though she wished to. Jhampri, always an eager participant in all such events of passing excitement, nearly danced with joy. "Where Moinadidi, where is it?"

At the burning ghat to the left of the village, the funeral pyre was burning. Naba Maiti had suffered for three months. The family had suffered with him. When he died, he took everything with him. The holy man could not do anything, neither could the doctor. At Egra, the Maitis were told that Naba had to be taken to either Contai or Kolkata. There was no treatment available in the village. Watching the smoke rise from the pyre, Moina remembered all this. The vultures waited atop the trees. Naba's elder brother placed a new towel and an earthen pot under the tree and threw a stone at the vultures. He had no eyes for the Parijan. Naba's father was poking the fire with a long pole. He worked at a tile kiln. It was his duty to see that there was enough fire for the tiles. The whole day he poked and jabbed at fire. Yet today his hands trembled as he thrust the long stick into the funeral pyre of his son.

Haguri looked around. There was fire in her eyes. Jhampri said, "Why do people die so young?"

"I do not know," said Haguri fiercely.

Moina said with impatience, "What are you waiting for? The Parijan will..."

Haguri shrank back. In this village, only they—only their family—had owned a palanquin. Today it was with Suren Jana. Four of his labourers had come to their house one fine morning and had carried away the empty Parijan. Haguri could not control herself that day. She had cried out in pain and humiliation. She thought they would get the Parijan back once Muchiya returned. But till now the Parijan had not returned. Never again would it rest in their verandah. Her old father had put his thumb impression on the white paper as Suren Jana pushed another rupee into his hands. Haguri remembered how still her father had stood then. After some time, he had taken the note. Jana had also offered him a cigarette and soothingly said, "This is just going from you to me. Just a change of hands. I hope you have no objection."

"Babu, can you get back something that you give away?"

Shrewd Suren Jana had left without a word.

Haguri was very quiet. Jhampri wiped the sweat off her face with the back of her hand and said, "What's wrong? Come on."

Haguri went unwillingly. She observed the palanquin: how grand and gorgeous it looked, how carefully it was decorated! Like a queen.

The palanquin would cross the burning ghat and reach Daudpur. Then it would return at night with the bride and the bridegroom.

The villagers would watch the firework display and listen to the loud jingles. While the dynamo rattled, Netai the Dancer would pin silver foil on his breast and dance to the rhythm of the loud music. The Jhumur band party would lead the procession with their love songs and accompanying dance, and all of this would keep the simple village folk spellbound.

Haguri could not check her tears.

Muchiya had returned after two months. Overcome by helplessness and rage at their misfortune, he had clutched at his scar with both hands and cried out, "O God!"

The palanquin trotted away along the Panchayati dam towards Daudpur. Haguri remained still and motionless. At Daudpur, Muchiya had bought for Moina a pair of big earrings and he hoped to keep this a secret from Haguri. He had given Haguri a parched rice cake.

Since that day, Haguri had nursed a bitterness against Moina which was not always apparent. Later she found out that Muchiya was in love with Moina. After the harvest, they wanted to elope and get married. Nobody in the village would support them. Moina's father would never agree to the marriage. Finally, nothing happened. Moina went away to Contai with her husband. Muchiya had kept standing under the arjun tree like a fool that day, as though he was rooted to the spot.

When the palanquin disappeared from sight, Jhampri said to Haguri, "Come on. What is the point in standing around? Shouldn't we go home?"

Haguri did not wish to go home. Her brother would surely ask, "Haguri, whose palanquin was it?" What would she tell him then? She had no words.

Haguri had never seen her brother healthy. He was always afflicted by something or the other. Once while returning from the weekly market, Muchiya's stomach ache had become so severe that his whole body had convulsed with pain. He had fallen down by the side of the canal, covered with sand. Some four or five field hands had taken him to the hospital in the scorching heat. He could be resuscitated that time thanks to the timely help.

The news had reached his aged father. He had prayed for his son's life and promised an offering to the deity. In a tearful voice he had said, "I promise you an offering. I will have music played during the offering ceremony. Give me back my son's life. You snatched away the palanquin, I said nothing. If you pluck out my eyes now, how will I survive? For what will I live?"

Haguri felt sad for her brother. He could not run. He could not lift any heavy weights; it left him panting for breath. If he ate even a handful of leftover rice, it produced a sour, acrid belch.

He felt constantly nauseous. The doctor had advised him not to eat anything that was sour, spicy or stale. But Muchiya loved to eat all kinds of sour pickles. He could eat a plate full of rice with only salt and chili. He had no likes and dislikes, he ate whatever he got. Once strong and muscular, his chest had contracted pathetically. It was easy to count his ribs, which protruded visibly under the skin. His stomach was always shriveled as though he was perpetually hungry. His bony jaws made him look ugly and old. Nobody would believe that he was only twenty-three, Muchiya had aged so quickly. Why else would there be dark circles around his eyes perpetually?

When their grandfather was alive, Haguri and Muchiya were so happy. There was no end to their fickle demands and unreasonable wishes, or to the amount of love and care they received. Whenever he went to the weekly market, he always brought *jilipi* for them and crisp roasted gram. Haguri and Muchiya would eat the crunchy, syrupy sweet as they played about. At times, Haguri would sit inside the Parijan and ask with wide-eyed curiosity, "Dadu, O Dadu! What is a Parijan?" The old man, who had seen both drought and flood, would be at a loss. Scratching his bald head, he would try to frame an answer, "It is what the bridegroom travels in when he goes to get married." But this answer would sound incomplete to his own ears. So rubbing his tongue over his gums, he would add, "The Parijan is a palanquin. A palanquin that is kept decorated and ready, and young girls like you set out in it for their husband's house, leaving their near and dear ones behind. While going away, they cry and cry."

The two sisters reached the banyan tree. This was the best place in the whole of Nanka-Hatida village. The leaves of the banyan tree had thinned due to the excessive heat. Sitting on its branches, a green pigeon and a parrot called out to their mates. The yellow banyan leaves fell twirling to the ground spinning like tops. The ground was so neat and smooth it seemed to have been mopped clean. There wasn't a blade of grass to be seen. Haritala was very close to the banyan tree. Its ancient, gnarled roots were testament to the time that had passed. The tulsi plant there stood lifeless. A drop or two of water fell from the hole made in the earthen pot.

Haguri left the communal tap behind and walked slowly to the pond owned by Sasmal. The rotten leaves that had accumulated on the surface of the pond had changed the colour of the water. It was neither green nor black. On peak summer days, when all the other ponds dried up, this pond helped the villagers. Haguri and Jhampri stood on the dry sand scrubbing their feet. They dipped the wicker basket into the water. A number of small *boshtami* fish summoned up courage and came close to the banks.

Haguri waded into the knee-deep water and carefully washed the greens they had collected. This was her whole day's earnings. She and the rest of the family would eat leftover rice with the fried greens. When they had the palanquin, they did not know scarcity. The money from renting out the palanquin on contract was enough. People from the surrounding ten or twelve villages came to their house every day. They spread out the mat and sat on the verandah smoking hookah and bargaining on the rate. Then followed the final offer in a sly turn of phrase and the final agreement. Finally, sharbat was served in glass tumblers. On the top would float the juicy pulp of the lemon. After having the sharbat, they would pick up the hookah again. The smell of raw tobacco would fill the corners of the courtyard, and Haguri would rest against the door like a brooding hen and listen to their conversation.

"Listen to me, Das, I haven't said anything wrong or unjustified," the chief of the other village would say, caressing his long beard.

"I cannot, babu. It is too little," Haguri's father would say with a shake of his head. "The decorations cost money. Plus I have to pay the six bearers. All the money is spent on this."

"Then you add another twenty-five."

"Excuse me, babu, but I cannot. You may go around looking, but you will not get another palanquin like this."

At long last the agreement would be drawn up. The old man would draw lines with a piece of charcoal on the wall to keep note of the time and day. On the appointed day, Muchiya would go along with the palanquin. His hair oiled and combed, Muchiya would lead the group. His whole body would be shining. A new towel lay folded on his left shoulder. In his right hand, he would carry a whip. Dressed in a new dhoti and kurta, he looked like a singer at the dance festival organised in honour of Lord Krishna.

Keeping the wicker basket on the bank, Haguri went down into the water again. She removed the leaves and weeds she had dipped in the water. Then shaking off the water from her hair with a jerk, she stood up straight. She filled her mouth with water and brushed her teeth with her finger. She rinsed her mouth and spit out the water in a spray. Jhampri, swimming underwater, had meanwhile reached the middle of the pond. Raising her head above the surface for a moment, she said, "You know, a big fish struck my foot with its tail just now and went away."

Haguri's eyes lit up at the mention of fish. It had been so long since they had tasted fish. How could they? Even the smallest fish cost thirty rupees a kilo. If Muchiya went to the weekly market, she would ask him to bring fish.

On returning home, Haguri saw Muchiya spreading out the thread for the net on the verandah. One fish net sold for about a hundred rupees. If he sold it, it would fetch him some money. Haguri went inside in the wet saree, dripping water all over the floor. She noticed that Muchiya ignored her and carried on with his work. He had stopped talking to Moina these days. He felt restless whenever he saw her.

"I'll bring a postcard to write a few lines. This is the last time," Moina had said, swallowing hard, as though trying to reassure herself of what she had said.

Muchiya had stopped his work and stared at Moina. "Give me the money."

On hearing Muchiya's dry words, Moina had given him twenty-five paisa. She had not been wearing a blouse; as she stretched out her hand, her heavy breasts and the curve of her shoulder had been exposed. Muchiya had put his hands on his hips and looked the other way.

Haguri was wearing her father's torn dhoti. She had only one saree and so when she washed it, she had nothing to wear. Muchiya's heart seemed to break. Cowering like an earthworm, he listened to the sounds of the cooking. On a fire made with the dried bark of the banana tree a large tumbler had been placed for cooking. The smell of the fried greens reached Muchiya. He felt hungry.

Moina, who came from a weaver's family, had sworn by Goddess Sitala, "I cannot live without you. If you are with me, I have no worry, no fear." All lies. Moina had told him only lies.

Muchiya frowned in anger and disgust. Moina was rubbing her back against the wall. Her back was covered with prickly heat.

"Is there any oil?" Muchiya asked Haguri. She passed the empty bottle to him, saying, "Do you know our palanquin went by the village today? Suren Jana went along. The eldest daughter of Muralibabu, who lives in Daudpur, is getting married today. They will return tonight."

"Shut up. Don't tell me anything about the palanquin."

Haguri did not stop. She kept on talking, as if under a spell, "How beautiful the palanquin looked! What decorations!" Muchiya could not breathe. Haguri had forgotten about the greens. The burnt smell reached his nostrils. Their father came in fanning himself with a towel and said, "What were you saying?"

Muchiya did not speak. His father kept on talking.

"Did you see the palanquin today? It went towards the big canal."

"I saw it," Haguri replied quickly and then looked at Muchiya. "The Janas have decorated the Parijan beautifully. People kept staring at it."

"Jana's palanquin?" Muchiya's fingernail seemed to dig into his scar. How did this small stomach of his digest the big palanquin? Muchiya looked up to see the sky. It was clear and blue. Suddenly he realised that he had not seen the sky in a long, long time.

He felt so lethargic these days. If he tried to laugh, his laughter broke midway like a rotten thread. Haguri tried to hide her feelings but could not. Her lips puckered up and her eyes filled with tears.

"What happened? Do you feel sad for the palanquin?"

Haguri was weeping, "Yes, I do. Even when mother died, I didn't feel so sad."

Muchiya did not go by the Panchayati canal road; he had taken a short cut. He carried a bottle to bring back oil. Haguri had told him there was nothing left. Oil, salt, chili—nothing. The container for the rice was also empty. If he managed to bring something back in the evening, only then could Haguri boil some rice. It was along this road that the palanquin had gone in the afternoon. Now there was no sign of it. Still Muchiya felt that Suren Jana was leading the way, and the six bearers were singing an indecent, wanton song.

Heyah, ho, ho, ho, ho! They trotted along the dusty road shaking their hands and heads. The bride and the bridegroom sat face to face in the palanquin in silence. They sat on a small handmade wooden throne that had pink flowers painted on it. Silken valances hung on the two open sides of the palanquin. The valances had beadwork on them and their fragrance could make one intoxicated. The smell of summer fields merged with that of the *attar* and became one.

Muchiya stumbled. He remembered Moina and the pale streak of vermillion in the parting of her hair. Dirt had accumulated on her conch bangles.

The postman had searched him out from the crowd at the weekly market and given him a postcard for Moina. It contained cruel, heart-rending words in big letters. It was written by Moina's husband. How could Muchiya give it to Moina? What if she did something? What if she killed herself? Who would look after Bishu then? He knew Moina's sensitive nature too well. For so little, she would uproot herself like a weed.

Evening was setting in. The fields, the huts, the trees—everything was being enveloped by a dark red veil descending from the sky. The last rays of the setting sun illuminated the nooks and corners of the land. Muchiya bought a salted fish. He got it pretty cheap. They had forgotten when they had last tasted fish. Everybody at Daudpur would eat to their heart's content at the marriage feast of Muralimohanbabu's daughter. Mutton would be served in plenty.

Muchiya walked quickly. It was by this route that the Parijan would return. Darkness spread over the empty fields. To see the palanquin at this hour, at this place would be nothing short of seeing a ghost. To jump into thorny bushes would be easier.

The local market was singing praises of Muralibabu. Suren Jana was swelling with pride and vanity. Everybody said that it had been a long time since they had seen such a well-decorated palanquin.

Dried, salted fish has a distinctive taste and flavour. Haguri asked her brother to go and call Moina. "Her son had been asking to eat fish. Tell her to come and eat with us."

Muchiya had forgotten the words of the letter. He read it again. He could feel the anger rising in his veins. He had not bought a postcard. What use was it anymore?

Haguri told him again to go to Moina. From the road that stretched itself along the canal came the sound of fireworks and bits of conversation. "The Parijan has come," said Haguri looking out into the dark, her ears alert and attentive.

"Oh, has it come already?" asked Muchiya, his voice sad and dispirited, "Will it go from here to the west block?"

"Yes, there is no other way," Haguri said.

Muchiya did not wait any longer. He went directly to the weaver's lane. The music came floating with the night breeze. He felt as though a wasp had stung him. He called out in desperation, "Moina! Ei Moina!"

The door opened, "Come, come inside."

For moments Muchiya stood still. Then on second thoughts he went inside. Moina heaved a heavy sigh.

"I think the bride has come."

"Perhaps."

They sat down. Bishu was fast asleep. A mosquito sat on his hungry stomach.

"How is it that you are here today?" Moina touched Muchiya's hand, "Won't people talk if you come to my house?"

Muchiya lit a *bidi*. Moina looked at him.

The marriage procession was approaching. The light of the petromax lit up the surrounding fields and the unmetalled path. Even the stones shone brightly in that light. The village had crowded near the communal tap to see the procession pass. A band was playing, crackers were burst. Jana pumped up the petromax. The bridegroom's father walked with measured steps holding a four-battery torch in hand and chewing *paan*. Netai the Dancer was dancing, cupping his hands over his ears.

Muchiya wanted to scream. He could not. Puzzled, Moina said, "What happened? What is it?"

"Come close. Come close to me." Muchiya was shivering. Moina could not read the language of his eyes. It was different. His breath smelled wild.

Moina tried to respond to his call. She knew that they loved each other still, yet she was hesitant to go close to him. It seemed as if her feet had grown roots that went deep down into the earth—she could not move. It was a strong desire battling against an even stronger grief and pain for her conch bangles and the pale vermillion line, the remnants of her marriage.

Translated by Anuradha Sen

THE PLUNDERER

The first thing I saw when I reached Chaibasa with my father was a hawk. It was circling high above us. Its shadow moved quickly towards the jungle. I stared at it in surprise. I had never seen a hawk from such close quarters before; I marvelled at the bird's power to soar so high and enjoy the proximity of the sun. We have a wood-apple tree in our courtyard. Sometimes in the afternoon and sometimes at dusk, I have seen a hawk sitting there, its head lowered towards the ground, its talons hooked to the bark of the tree. Mother always said that the hawk is ruthless—it has no sympathy or concern for other lives. I asked her about vultures. Ma said vultures only frequented the dump yards for carrion. They did not snatch away live things like the hawk did.

I remembered my mother's words the moment I set foot on Chaibasa's red soil. I remembered the huge grey hawk that came and sat panting on the wood-apple tree. Ma said that a hawk, whether asleep or awake, is always plotting how best to kill its prey. It is determined to achieve its aim and always has its eye on its objective.

I have always sensed in my mother's words a certain danger, of something unknown. Something which has also pervaded me. I suddenly felt very thirsty. Timidly, I asked my father how far we were from Balidihi.

Perhaps Baba had not heard my question. He was busy with the cycle on the roof of the bus. I did not ask him again. I feared that my question might distract him. Travelling by a direct bus would have been a lot of trouble. I knew that very well. So we could not reach Balidihi directly from Chakradharpur without a break. We had to stop at Chaibasa, Kuju and Ichhapur. The rickshaw fare for the connecting routes was too much. And so to save the money, Baba brought the cycle along. Back home, Ma had tried to stop him, to reason with him, but no. He would take the cycle along. He curtly brushed aside all her advice.

"How will you understand the value of money? You don't earn it. Only those who do so with the sweat of their brow know its value."

His scornful words drained her mind of peace that pleasant morning.

I am now sixteen. I will sit for the Madhyamik Examination this year. I can understand how important money is, though I have never felt the need for it. I did not like the idea of dragging the cycle along either. My father's desire to save a meagre amount of money reminded me of the story of the close-fisted old man. I don't know why, but as I looked at my father now, it seemed that a hawk had alighted on his shoulders. His dhoti and shirt, washed and starched and ironed, looked uglier than a hawk's ugly feathers. What was that spot on the sleeve? Time and again, and much against my will, my eyes reverted to that black spot.

It was not easy for my father to get the cycle down from the roof of the bus. The delay irritated the bus *khalasi*. He told my father to move away.

"Get out of the way. Why did you climb up if you don't have the strength?" he screamed. And then he threw down the cycle which fell on the ground with a loud clang.

My father shrank away like a guilty man. Sadly, he turned towards me and smiled a pale, meaningless smile. He said, "Parimal, are you hungry? There are many good shops here. They sell good sweets."

I wasn't hungry and I told him so. Ma had served us a full meal before we left. Just a one-hour journey could not have made me hungry. At that moment however, I thought of my mother. In a mournful voice she had told me, "Your grandfather had lived in the village that you are going to. Two generations of your ancestors lived in that house which is now in a dilapidated condition. Of course, nobody lives there today. Everybody has left for the town, secure in the thought that a life of plenty awaits them there." Whenever mother spoke to me about the village and our ancestors, she could not control herself. In her sorrow she looked like an uprooted tree. I could not understand the reason for her sorrow. Didn't Ma know that life sped along with time? It always did. Then why couldn't she overcome the pain of recollection?

This was my first visit to Chaibasa. This year, the centre for the Madhyamik Examination will be at Chaibasa. My friend and I will have to stay there then. My mother will come with us.

Baba covered some distance with great difficulty. Heaving a deep sigh, he wiped his face with the end of his dhoti and said, "How will we go? My eyes are burning in the hot sun." He raised his hand to shade his eyes. Looking at him, I felt sorry for Baba. The distance between Chaibasa and Kuju is just eight kilometres. Covering these eight kilometres seemed to be a Herculean task. The road shimmered in the heat. My father stood undecided under the shade of a tree and lit a *bidi*. As he drew in a long smoke, his sharp jawline became more apparent. His face seemed so ugly and Baba looked so miserably old.

Baba finished the bidi. He looked at the road that lay bare and empty before us and said, "Sit. Hold me tightly. Mind you don't fall."

The hot, fatigued breath of the earth that had brushed against our skin only a moment ago suddenly surrendered to the shade of the sheesham-sal-peepal trees. The road in front of our house was also lined with trees. But their shade didn't feel like the soft caress I felt now. This time of the year, heatwaves wreaked havoc. When I returned from school, my polished shoes and my school bag would be covered with dust. I would draw lines on them.

Father said, "Drawing lines on the dust made one a debtor." Mother said, "Writing on the dust is wrong. When you do so, all learning mingles with the dust. Nothing remains."

The cycle speeded along, leaving everything by the road far behind. The caressing shade of the dense forest spread upon my thoughts too. I began weaving dream upon dream. I could not remember if I had seen such a dense jungle before. The one that we crossed while going to my maternal uncle's house was nothing compared to this. The faster the cycle raced, the more I lost myself in thoughts. Holding on tightly to the rod of the cycle, I gazed intently at faraway villages where pallid, haggard village girls walked along the ridges of fields with bunches of dried twigs balanced upon their heads. Clad in striped multicoloured sarees, they trudged on, defying the hot, steel-white sun. The bright hues of their clothes brought to my mind happy, fond memories. Baba said, "Those girls live in the village nearby; they have nothing to do and so they frequent the jungles. They hoodwink the keeper and take away the *kendu* and the sal leaves. They steal *mahua* seeds which they sell in the local market. The money helps them."

I said, "They are very poor, aren't they?" My father looked at me sternly. Then he said cuttingly, "Do they have to steal just because they are poor? Steal just to satisfy their needs?"

I kept quiet. But Baba continued.

"They live in poverty, but does that mean they can do whatever they want? The jungles belong to the government. Nobody can claim even a handful."

Our Bengali teacher had told us about the Adibasis.

"Adibasis are the aboriginal inhabitants of the earth. They are the primitive forest dwellers. The Arya Samaj had kept them away in fear and hatred. The jungle is the stage on which the drama of their life, from birth, through childhood, adolescence and youth to old age, unfolds. Yet, surprisingly, they are driven out of these very jungles by the law. They have been treated with utter contempt and neglected since the days of British rule. And the extreme disregard they face is still not over."

I couldn't understand who was right: my father or my teacher? I was astonished to see the poverty and ignorance that prevailed among the Adibasis. No one should know such humiliation! I did not know that such extreme poverty still existed.

I had been sitting on the carrier of the cycle for quite some time. My hips ached. My legs had been suspended for so long that they had become numb. I was forced to tell my father to stop. He looked around and then stopped under a tree. I could once again see the pallid village girls. Disregarding the harshness of the sun, they walked in a straight line and covered long distances at a fast pace. They looked like neglected angels. The wind raised a whirlpool of dust. Their bangles and the twigs they carried were coated with the red dust from the road. Their sarees were stained with the malicious red of the gravel. It was not the revelry of Lord Krishna's feast but the pathetic picture of their daily struggle, the struggle for existence. The cruel sun blazed down upon the spot where we were standing. Baba was breathing in a strange way with his mouth open. I turned my eyes away from his sickly angular face.

I looked around. The scorching summer day had a harshness of its own. Yet from within the harshness trickled a soft delicate beauty—so soft, so peaceful, that it seemed to flow from the tranquil heavens above.

I gazed on and on, infatuated. My eyes longed to drink deep the beauty of this red soil. Fascinated, I asked Baba the name of the tree under which we were standing. He smiled an indulgent smile and replied, "Kusum. Haven't you seen it before?"

"Kusum flowers are beautiful," said Baba in a slow and serious voice. "White flowers adorn the tree and their sweet fragrance soothes and relaxes. Oil is extracted from the seeds."

"Who uses the oil?"

My question at once brought back the dissatisfaction and anger to his face. He turned to look at the village, deprived of its grace and glory. Our Bengali teacher had told us about the seeds of the sal and mahua. "Kusum, mahua, sal and neem seeds are oil seeds. The village folk are habituated to using them. But now they have no claim whatsoever on the forest products. The Forest Department has leased the forest to sub-contractors. Their staff come and pluck all the seeds every year. Truckloads of seeds are then sent to the towns and cities. The hapless villagers can only stand and stare." Sir had continued, "This is a kind of torture. This is time's tragedy. A time will come when these people will rise up in protest against their oppressors. Only then will the roots of exploitation be snapped."

I have often heard about Birsa Munda, the legendary hero. Once at the Birsa Mela, a fair held at Chakradharpur, I listened in awe to the tales of his courage and bravery from a tribal youth. I had then felt that Birsa was not an ordinary human but God. My mother too supported my opinion.

An old Adibasi woman works in our house. Her appearance bore the distinct signs of poverty. My mother always gave her the leftover rice and chapatis, which she took home happily. Her grandson wore the shirts and pants I discarded and handed down. He is about my age but so pathetically thin. I have often seen these hapless people drinking rice beer. Ma said there was nothing wrong in it. The rice beer kept them alive. Where would they have the money to buy lemons and curd to cool themselves in this tremendous heat? My father had a different opinion. He said, "That fellow is a thief, and quite an expert at that."

My mother did not share his opinion. She believed it was our hatred, our contempt and ill treatment that had robbed them of their essential goodness.

Strangely enough, Baba never tolerated Ma's views though he never said anything to that effect. He would stare at the Adibasis' tumbledown huts at such moments. I have seen lines of worry appearing on his forehead as an uninvited fear settled in his eyes.

My uncle is a hard-hearted person. He runs his business at Lotapur. During the off-season, he never fails to buy kendu leaves from the Adibasis at a throwaway price. The same leaves when sold during season brought in thrice the amount of profit. My uncle is now a rich man. He has a double-storeyed house. A motorcycle too. He rides it to town to transact business with the moneylender. Flushed with success, he likes to narrate stories of the pathetic life of the Adibasis. One story in particular left an indelible mark on me. Since that day I have looked upon my uncle as a ruthless monster.

There was a young Adibasi mother with a bundle of kendu leaves on her head and her seven-month-old suckling at her waist, tied to her with a towel. The baby was crying for milk. My uncle did not offer the mother a drop of milk. Instead, he bought the leaves from her at a throwaway price and showed her the tea stall. As luck would have it, there was no milk available. The mother had to finally dip her finger in a cup of tea, cool it and then feed her baby the tea, drop by drop.

My uncle had no shame at all. He had no regret in being the cause of such a disgraceful event. On the contrary, his words and manners bore unmistakable signs of pride, of belonging among the feudal lords. He boasted that he knew very well how to fool them. He maliciously added that the longer the Adibasis remained illiterate, the better it was for him, and then he burst out laughing. My father supported my uncle's go-getter attitude with a faint smile.

Ma, flushing with shame and anger, had spoken up, "Always remember: if you are evil unto others, evil will come back at you. God keeps a record of everything. He will return your dues in due course with interest."

It took us about an hour to reach Ichhapur. Just a mile more, I told myself, and then we will reach our village and see the house. Our abandoned and dilapidated house. My grandfather had left the village some fifty years ago when he got a job in the town. He knew Sanskrit and was a reputed teacher. The Singhdeo Rajas had given him about fifty acres of land.

As a devout Brahmin and teacher of Sanskrit, my grandfather had earned respect from all and sundry. Yet what greed urged him to leave his ancestral village is a mystery. My mother said nothing. My questions only brought tears to her eyes. She assured me that I would get to know everything when I grew up. What she meant by 'growing up', I don't know. But I feel I am mature enough to discuss such matters. If not, would my father have brought me along? I didn't want to accompany him. Ma had not wanted it either.

"He can go some other time," she had said. "There is a meeting at Chaibasa today. The buses will be too crowded."

"Forget meetings," shouted my father. "Do we have to sit back at home because of it? You and your womanly wisdom!"

My mother had looked at him in surprise. His harsh words left her shaken.

Then, in a sad voice Baba had said, "I have had two heart attacks. I feel my days are numbered. I can no longer cope with the stress of looking after our landed property. Let him take stock of all that we have. He has nobody to stand by him."

We have fifty acres of land in the nearby poverty-stricken village. Previously, my father used to go on a monthly visit. Now, with old age settling in, he has cut down his visits. He goes there once a year to claim his share of the harvest. After the Pujas, it is difficult for him to remain calm. He spends his time dreaming about the rice fields. His profound regrets find expression in the accusations he hurls at my mother, as though she were his staunch enemy. He would look at her in doubt and disbelief and brush aside whatever she said. Then he would scribble down a few lines—

"To Nona Samad,

Be ready. We are reaching on the 4th of November. I want my share on that day itself. You will be in trouble if you fail to give it."

My father's aggressive and authoritative nature was apparent in each letter that he wrote. It was something I could never accept. He nurtured a deep-rooted grudge against Nona Samad. It seemed to me that our house—nay, even the walls—became vocal in their grudge against him. Perhaps it was for this reason that I came to know him well and to look upon Nona Samad as a member of our family. Baba had, of course, never accepted him as one. He never missed a chance to abuse Nona Samad. To him, Nona was a thief, a devil who cheated him out of his rightful share. Who grew fat and healthy while my father had to buy rice at five rupees a kilo.

Unable to endure such mean words, my mother said one day that Baba could not claim anything from Nona or the land for that matter. He should be satisfied with whatever he got. She was right. My father had willingly sold the land at a reasonable rate to the government for the proposed construction of the Ichha-Kharkhaiya dam that was yet to begin. But my father took advantage of Nona Samad's ignorance and still took his share of the harvest. I wonder if he understood how pathetic his egoistical behaviour was. Old Nona Samad did not understand the legal rules and regulations. So with complete sincerity and devotion, he gave my father his share.

Father was livid with Ma. He shouted back, "*You* say this! How dare you? For shame! Who am I keeping house with—a traitor?"

Ma had no courage left after this unfortunate incident. My father's cruel words cut her deep. She looked at me and could not hold back the despondent tears that rolled down her cheeks.

I don't like to see Ma sad. I know my mother is nobler than any of the female characters depicted in our epics. When all was well, she often told me a story. My grandfather was a railway servant. He had no fixed hours of duty because he was a guard. My grandmother having died at childbirth, there was no one to look after the infant. Finally, the wife of an Adibasi porter came to the rescue. She was my mother's wet nurse. Ma always spoke of her with respect and gratitude.

The cycle raced along, raising clouds of red dust that engulfed us. All of a sudden, a sweet fragrance wafted in and made me restless. We were passing by a mango tree. A gentle breeze laden with the sweet fragrance of the first mango blossoms washed over me. Before I had time to recover from the effect, I saw an Adibasi boy, nearly naked, trying to break a twig from a neem tree. He looked at us in bewilderment. The neem trees stood tall and straight, covered with small, white flowers. The friendly breeze carried their delicate fragrance to faraway places.

My father said, "The shade of the neem tree and this breeze is good for health."

I smelt the fragrance and the pain.

"Then why is that boy so thin?" I asked. Father looked at me with displeasure. "Oh! So you too know how to speak. Will you also follow in your mother's footsteps?"

At last we reached Nona Samad's house. Before father could ring the cycle bell, a good-looking peasant girl came running out.

She was about my age, and was wearing a faded violet blouse and a sheet wrapped around her body like a dhoti. She looked at me and smiled. Then flushing with embarrassment, she bent her head down like a brooding hen. A silver necklace complemented her dark beauty and soft face. The rays of the afternoon sun fell upon her cheeks and forehead, making her look even more graceful. The multi-coloured glass bangles that covered her smooth wrists produced a melancholic sound. She looked up at father once, and then at me, and ran away. Her black, wavy hair swung in rhythm with her movement.

Baba heaved a long and deep sigh. Looking at me he said in a low voice, "Just look at that, silver ornaments! All of this with the money they get by selling my grains. I feel I have to go back empty-handed."

I didn't like my father's coarse, cruel remarks. They hurt my self-respect. I turned my face away. Seeing me remain silent, he asked, "Are you thirsty?"

I nodded.

"Nona comes from a low caste. We cannot accept water from his hands. Take out a lozenge," he told me.

I did not need it. I bit my lip and looked the other way. That my father was so blindly orthodox and superstitious shocked me. I couldn't even look at him. But he was staring at me, his peering eyes trying to read my thoughts.

Baba said to me after sometime, "Go and stand under the *karam* tree. I'll see if Samad is at home. It's likely that he isn't. This is the trouble in sending a letter. They will go off to Chaibasa under some pretext. Yet your mother says they are simple and innocent."

Before my father could finish, old Samad, bent with age, hurried over, supporting himself with a stick. He bent down to touch my father's feet. Baba allowed him to do so. As far as I knew, the young touched the feet of the elders. Here it was just the opposite.

Then Samad brought a charpoy from somewhere and placed it under the shade of the karam tree. My father went and sat on it with the arrogance of a master. Old Samad stood in front of him, head bowed, sweating and rubbing his hands. There was a slave-like docility in his manners. He composed himself and then called out, "Ei Sombari! Sombari, get a fan."

Sombari, who had only a moment ago looked me in the eyes, came out with a hand-fan, her face flushed crimson with embarrassment. Samad told her, "Take care of our honoured guests. They have come from far. I am going to draw water. And tell your mother to crack a wood-apple to make sharbat."

Samad went away while Sombari continued to fan us. Sometimes she looked at us, wide-eyed with wonder. How were her eyes so large and bright? Perhaps she had applied kohl. My mother used to apply it to my eyes when I was a child. She would say, "Kohl is good for the eyes. It is the eyes' best friend. It helps to develop a good and powerful vision." I couldn't understand then what mother meant by 'powerful vision'. Today I understood what it meant as I gazed intently at her large, dark eyes.

Baba also stared. Not at Sombari of course, but at the neat and clean courtyard. Swabbed with cow-dung, it had a smooth brightness that put cemented floors to shame. Then he looked at the haystack in the corner. Ma and I had often heard my father proclaim proudly that he could ascertain how good the harvest was by looking at the hay. He was calculating—and I could say this with confidence—nothing else but his due. Sometimes an unrestrained excitement flooded his face.

Baba and I washed our hands and feet with the cool water that Samad had brought for us. Baba wiped his feet with Samad's new towel and then left it under the charpoy. It lay there, covered with dust. Old Nona observed everything helplessly. Finally, he said, "Malik, let me bring you a glass of sharbat. The wood-apples of my tree are sweet as honey."

Father shrieked, "No, no. I am fasting."

"Chhota Malik, please accept a glass of sharbat."

I looked at my father who stared back. "No!" his eyes seemed to say. The old man looked at us. Poor man! His smiling face contorted with worry. He sighed and sat down on the ground, face to face with my father. They chatted about the village and the town, the hot summer days, the drought, the insects, the festivals and so on. My eyes were searching for Sombari. Suddenly she appeared with a packet of cigarettes and a matchbox on a brass plate. Old Samad smiled. Pushing the plate towards my father, he said, "Here, Malik. Have a smoke."

Father lit a cigarette and said, "It will not be wise to wait. Measure out my share. I will have to set out at sundown. It's quite a distance." His strong and commanding voice sounded like that of the zamindars. Samad shifted in his seat and said, "All right, I will give you your share. But babu, the produce has been very scanty. No rain, babu. The land and the rocks... everything has cracked."

Father hissed, "Every year it is the same story. Enough of excuses! Show me the grain."

Old Samad stared at father sadly. The destitute labourer's condition would have brought tears to the eyes of even the most unsympathetic person. Baba softened a little, "Well, what have you decided?"

Samad raised all ten fingers four times. It was enough to make my father lose his temper. He stood up in anger and snarled at Samad who stood by like a beast of burden.

"Only forty! Not even one mound per acre. Is there no law? Just leave. I will find someone else to till the land. I am an old Brahmin. Do you think you will live in peace if you cheat me?"

The last sentence brought a visible change upon Samad. I saw on his face an emptiness that I had not expected. And that set me thinking. Samad ploughed the field, sowed the seeds, reaped the harvest with his unceasing toil and labour, but got very little in return. Throughout his life he has been enduring hardships. And at last he is asked to leave. Deprived not only of all the things one needed in life, but also of his self-respect. Finally, after some time, he spoke like one who has lost the battle, "You deserve another ten, babu, but I cannot give it. We went through hard times. There was a dearth of food. We had nothing else to eat. Punish me, I will not say anything."

My father said, "Who are you trying to fool with all this?"

Samad bent his head in shame. Yet my father continued, "I haven't seen a man greedier than you in Singhbhum. You devour what belongs to others." Still Samad remained silent. My father's anger knew no bounds. He screamed in a shrill voice, "Answer me. You are not that innocent. Don't think I will spare you, the thief that you are."

Samad looked up. Years of intense labour showed on his face and made him look older. In a voice that shook with emotion he said, "Babu, I am not a thief or a plunderer. I am a human being."

"I can see that very well," my father said sarcastically, "But you belong to the jungle."

"There were jungles, babu, once upon a time. Not anymore. It's all been snatched away."

"Quiet! Stop talking like the leaders. You have nothing to eat and yet you talk big." Baba started coughing and I could see tears in the corners of Samad's eyes. He wiped his eyes and agreed to forty-five.

Samad spread out a mat. A big balance hung securely from a triangular structure made with bamboo poles.

My father came closer to observe. The husband and wife brought basket after basket of grain from the granary. And I could see that every time they did so, they were boiling with wrath. Their eyes glowed in anger and sent sparks of fury on to the grain. I shuddered and shifted my glance towards Sombari, only to see a helpless, morose look on her face. She stood there for some time and then ran away.

Avoiding my father's eyes, I followed her like a coward. Sombari had by then climbed up a drumstick tree. I looked admiringly at the clear footprints she left on the heap of ash below. On the day of the full moon in the month of Ashwin, my mother would draw such neat little footprints on the floor. For on that day, Lakshmi, the Goddess of Wealth, visited every house.

Sombari's laughter broke my train of thought. Her laughter was as musical as the music of the *jaltaranga*; it flowed in ripples.

When she found me standing there foolishly, Sombari grew bold. Wiping her forehead, she said, "Malik, pick up the drumsticks. Take them home. Your mother likes them."

I picked them up one by one. As I did so, I realised Nona and his family were poor in terms of wealth but richer than the richest so far as magnanimity was concerned. Sombari came down and stood by me. I don't know why, but my legs began trembling violently and drops of sweat trickled down my moustache.

Others were busy weighing and measuring out the grain. Meanwhile, a delicate shade had spread itself over the village. Sombari smiled at me, "Come, Chhota Malik. Let me show you our village. Do you know at the far end there is a river that girdles the village like a necklace? If you wish, I can show you around."

Together we set out. Everything was so jubilant. The birds cried in delight as they flew around in circles. We walked on under the tall trees by the side of the bushes, the scattered tufts of short grass and then the river appeared in front of us. I heard the sound of the river beating against its sides, crashing on the banks. I stood there watching the river's fury—as if it was trying to break free from all restrictions. The weather was perfectly clear and we could clearly see every wave. The beauty of the river invoked a sense of fear and disturbed my mind. I didn't know that a river could be so radiant with pride and glory. It flowed on to meet the roaring deep. Had I ever seen such beauty before? The bohemian breeze brought with it the sweet perfume of neem and mahua blossoms. An undefinable feeling tore my heart. We left paradise for hell. Realising how right my mother was, my eyes filled with tears. My father seemed to me a usurper. The money from the sale of lands kept as a fixed deposit in the bank brought in a huge interest, nearly four times more than his salary. Yet, he wasn't satisfied. Meanwhile old Nona toiled on government land and gave my father his share, year after year. My father oppressed and exploited this simple, honest, hardworking Nona who had been reduced to an animal as the victim of a lasting struggle for biological survival.

Sombari and I stood there on the brown land. Her joy knew no bounds for having brought me here. She seemed lively as the flowing river. She spread out her hands and said, "Ha Chhotobabu, look at the land! It's all yours! How rich you are! How very rich!"

On our way back, she stopped me under a tree and asked me the name of the tree. I looked up and saw the sky—a clear blue!

Sombari laughed, "You couldn't answer, babu. I knew you wouldn't be able to. You live in the town."

"What tree is it?"

Chewing on a dry leaf, Sombari said, "Mahua. See how beautiful the flowers are! How sweet the fragrance is!" She paused. Then, suddenly serious, she said, "In the summer, the mahua helps us survive, babu. It is intoxicating."

When Sombari was speaking, I looked around and saw a few village boys and girls. They were observing me carefully. I saw traces of fear in their eyes. They pointed towards me as they spoke among themselves. Everything about them was different. Their attitude was unbearable.

I beckoned them to come nearer, hoping to make friends. There was no other way to save myself from their razor-sharp eyes. I walked towards them.

"*Komboo, Komboo!*" they said and ran away in fear. Then they stopped abruptly and looked at me once again in terror and loathing.

This sudden turn of events left me speechless. I tried to call them back, "Listen! Listen, brother." But they did not. They ran to a safe distance, raising clouds of red dust behind them. Tears blinded my vision. That word was like poison. Sombari said in a low voice, "Come, babu."

I said, "Sombari, what is the meaning of 'Komboo'?"

Sombari hesitated. I held her hands firmly and said, "So you will not tell me. All right. I will never come to your village again."

I don't know what meaning my words carried, but Sombari started crying. Then after sometime she said, "Babu, it means plunderer. Those who loot and plunder everything—grain, animal, land... everything."

The gentle, friendly breeze carrying Nona's tired voice reached me, "Twenty-one, twenty-two... Komboo, Komboo, Komboo..."

Translated by Anuradha Sen

THE RELEASE

Nidhu was a *Dom* by birth. For hours he had been trying to find a corpse and was nearly half-dead with fatigue himself. He felt that his reputation was imperilled now. Like a fish, he had been gliding smoothly and continuously through the water, creating small, delicate ripples. His hands and feet had turned wrinkled and white, his fingers were severely cramped and he was shivering. But his ordeal was still not over. People had gathered in large numbers near the bamboo grove. The news had spread like wildfire. There was no end to the excitement and conjecture. And why wouldn't they be excited? The man who had come to murder Ranababu had fallen into the village pond. His corpse had to be found. So Nidhu was given the job. If he failed, the fishermen from the neighbouring villages would come. They would throw their nets; perhaps luck would favour them. But then, Nidhu's prestige would be ruined. After all, he was no ordinary man. He became desperate now. Although he was subjected to much physical suffering, he did not care. He did not think of giving up the search. Yes, he would dive in once again and rummage through the water. If he found the corpse, well and good. If not, it would seem that fate was against him.

Seeing Nidhu standing, the constable gave him a push and said, "Go, go on. Why are you wasting your time?" Nidhu looked at him in disgust. He could not tolerate such orders. He had spared no pains. Yet he could not spot the corpse. What could he do? He couldn't die for it, could he? He was tired to the very bones.

The sun on his back was too strong. Nidhu could feel his whole body burn. He could hear, amidst the din and confusion, the repeated wild thudding of his heart.

Nidhu walked away from there. He stood under a *jeol* tree for some time. Then he dived headlong into the water. He swam on and on, intoxicated by the smell of the water and the greenery in it.

It had been raining in torrents the night before. Owing to the cold winds and the torrential rain, there was nobody around. The sound of the gunshots reached far. Everyone had heard it clearly, not once but twice. The lights were out. Ranababu had fainted. Sensing danger, the man had run away. Down the water pipe, and off he had run. The big broad-muzzled dog had chased him, determined to tear into bits the man who dared to attack his master. But the dog fell dead near the gate, shot by the man who jumped over the compound wall and ran. The sound of his heavy and hurried footsteps could be heard clearly in the silence of the night. The unmetalled road was submerged in water. But nevertheless, he ran, followed by some four or five people. Lightning flashed across the sky once again. In the brief blinding flash of light, he saw the dense bamboo clumps and steered himself towards them for shelter. The people following him stopped. They looked at each other, undecided. They did not dare to enter the bamboo clumps even in broad daylight. And at night, especially a night turned frightful by thunder and lightning, it was out of question. It was not a very nice place. During daytime many figures moved about in that shadowed gloom. Oh God! Who knows what moves about there during the night hours?

They stood there and before they could turn back, they heard the unmistakable sound of someone falling headlong into water.

The splash was followed by a heart-rending cry. The people stopped dead in their tracks as the sound reached them. A few stars peeped out and the fireflies played about in the darkness. Like the sound of insects, bits of conversation floated in the air.

"Into the water."

"He will swim to safety."

"Come on, it's not easy."

"He had a gun."

"Yes, he told you so."

Nidhu reached the middle of the pond. He wanted out. He could not keep up any longer. A long-term habit of smoking and drinking had taken its toll. He longed for a bowl of his homemade rice beer that would give him the strength and tenacity required for such jobs. One could not—Nidhu reasoned with himself—do such a job without it. But the sepoybabus did not understand all this. The policeman standing under the shade of the arjun tree kept on shouting like a parrot, "Nidhu, *jaldi*, hurry up! Very soon it will get dark!"

What does it matter to me, thought Nidhu. He could not afford to die in the process of finding Ranababu's assailant. The babus were always in a hurry. This was not child's play.

On reaching the middle of the pond, Nidhu looked around in wonder. Were there so many people in the village? All of them stood close together. The leaves of the water hyacinth glistened and their lustre attracted the bees. They came and sat on the pale blue flowers.

Suddenly, Nidhu was aware of something biting him. He pulled out the leech on his thigh and turned around and swam on, holding the bamboo pole. The pond was full of water reeds but where was the corpse? Will he fail? Will he then bring shame to his father's and grandfather's reputation? In desperation he dived in again. He worked with more care and precision this time. At the point where the shadow of the arjun tree ended, Nidhu stopped for a moment. He was too tired; he drew in a long, deep breath and sensed something immediately. He could not dive. He turned his glance carefully, very carefully so as not to miss anything. His nose took in every smell. Holding the pole, Nidhu started swimming on his back. Then as he swam on, his head struck against something. Nidhu thought it was a pole and decided to swim on. But then he saw it. The body was covered all over by the water reeds and only the head was visible. It had thick black hair.

Nidhu squealed like a rabbit and then shouted. The police on duty helped him to lift up the body that was heavy and swollen. The chowkidar raced to the police station. The news had to reach the superintendent of police. Ranatosh Bhuniya was the local MLA. A murder attempt on him was no joke.

Having fought to the limits of his strength, Nidhu could no longer control himself. Like an old, worn-out ox, he sat with his tongue out, panting for breath, and stared into the distance with unseeing eyes. Then as he looked at the corpse, his eyes widened in recognition and he exclaimed, "Oh no! He looks so much like Tapobabu!" Nidhu did not know what to do. He sat there motionless. Nidhu had nothing to lose in life. Whatever he earned he spent on cheap pleasures. He thought of the days when he and his wife had tried every kind of herb, hoping for a child. But all was in vain. The agony and humiliation was too much for his wife. She died all too soon leaving Nidhu alone. He had been alone ever since, deprived of hope, love and all other emotions that helped human beings survive.

Nidhu had the experience needed for the job. He knew very well the difference between a simple and a critical case. So he had said nothing in reply. He looked in contempt at the officers who feared being terminated from service at the failure to solve every trivial case. As the S.P. abused them over the telephone, their fear increased by leaps and bounds. People said Ranababu was an epitome of kindness. Why then did someone wish to kill him? Rumours always irritated Nidhu. He had known Ranababu and his family since childhood. Ranababu's grandfather was a zamindar. The young maidens and brides of the village feared to go to the pond. Lata was murdered by him. He had looted her maidenhood and then thrown her body into the well. Her father was silenced with only a fourth of an acre of land. The same blood ran in Ranababu's veins, now a big, important man in the village. Powerful and rich, Ranababu had spent a full lakh on his daughter's wedding.

Nidhu started sweating. His spine ached. Did he not have any self-respect? The officer-in-charge at the police station had abused him and also accused him of being a spy. He had thundered, "I will throw you out of your job! I will make you a beggar, you rascal, you son of a pig trying to be a spy. I'll finish you!"

Many in the village could not tolerate Tapobabu. But he was a good man. Once Ranababu had broken Haladhar's balance because Haladhar had refused to sell him fish for twelve rupees instead of twenty; how could he dare refuse Ranababu? It was Tapobabu who had protested then. He had also extracted the money for the loss from the big man, who had then gone into the tea stall with his head bent low.

Nidhu did not possess such courage. He did not protest. Perhaps this is why he admired Tapobabu. Had he been as bold as Tapobabu, he would not have endured all the abuses denigrating his parents hurled at him every now and then. Actually, hunger was responsible for his lack of courage. It seemed to Nidhu that he had become a slave to this overpowering hunger that cost him his self-respect. Of course, his father was not innocent. To a certain extent he too was responsible. Why didn't he dare to protest? What was the use of his hefty physique then?

Sitting there by the pond, Nidhu started abusing his dead father, "Just come down once, I will pull apart your limbs and dry them in the sun for you. Who are you to dictate my life?" Staring at the dead body, Nidhu vacillated between anger and sorrow. He could not understand why he was feeling this way. This had not happened to him before. He would go to the district to help his father deal with corpses even before he was an adolescent. He used to sit like a statue by the side of the dead. His father never failed to encourage him in such moments, "Do not be afraid, my son. Keep a small piece of iron with you. Tie it to your upper arm for safety, and nobody will dare to come near you."

Hiding his face between his knees, Nidhu would hear his father say, "What is there to fear about the dead? They cannot breathe, they cannot speak. Always remember, it is not the dead but the living who stab you from behind. The dead are cold. They don't move, they don't fight."

But his father's words could not assuage his fears. To make things worse, his father was a drunkard. He often boasted that no one could do what he did. It was no gentleman's job. One had to be bold to do the work.

Nidhu had become an addict at an early age. Observing his behaviour, his shrewd father had told him, "Do not look at young girls. They are very cunning, son. They will rob you of your physical strength and vitality." There was no harm in looking at a man though. But his father must have lied. If not, then why did Tapobabu's dead body, a man's body, disturb him so? Nidhu observed Tapobabu. The shirt on him was ragged and exposed his upper body. His blue trousers clung to his ankles. His eyes were half closed, and his teeth were broken like old tombstones in a ghastly cemetery.

The grass soaked up the water as the sun shone with all its might. Everything sparkled. The tall bamboo swayed in the wind, making a melancholy sound. Nidhu's starved stomach growled for food. Right then, two other policemen came chewing *paan*. Nidhu stood up, swaying on his feet. "Look," he said, staring innocently, "I think he was a good man, sir."

The police laughed at him. Nidhu shrank back in fear. Back at the police station the officer had questioned him regarding the whereabouts of Kartikbabu's second son. The question was not at all simple. Nidhu had scratched his head and replied cautiously, "Sir, he studies in Kolkata. A very good boy. I have known him since his childhood, sir."

The officer kept quiet for some time and then he said slowly, "Times are bad. If you meet him, tell him not to get involved in any controversy. There are many reports against him."

Nidhu had warned Tapobabu accordingly that very day. But he was not one to listen. Brushing the matter aside, a defiant Tapobabu had told Nidhu, "I will speak the truth. Whatever the consequences be, I will speak. I am not afraid of the police."

Nidhu did not drag it on. The village folk doubted Nidhu. Everybody took him to be a spy of the police. But not Tapobabu. How could one wish to kill a man like him? How could one wish misfortune on such a man? Nidhu knew the officer was not a nice man. Utterly selfish, he did not even spare his own son. Nidhu was terribly scared of him.

Nidhu did not understand Tapobabu's ways. He was always busy with his books. He had no time to shave his face. His thin body lacked lustre, although his sharp retorts were sharper than an arrow thrust into one's soul.

Kartikbabu had asked Nidhu to look after his son, Tapo. He could not understand the change that had come over his son. Tapo stayed back in the village. He did not return to the hostel as he was a suspect there too. His education was lost in the labyrinth of politics. But Kartikbabu could not say anything to his motherless son. He did not know how to talk to someone so serious and so withdrawn. So the father avoided his son as much as he could. He only observed him from a distance.

Tapobabu had dragged the village chief by the collar and slapped him. This had led to a police case. He had been released on certain conditions. The MLA had also warned Kartikbabu, a reputed teacher. Perhaps it was his father's reputation that had saved Tapobabu for the time being. Yet he paid no heed to all this.

His friends from Kolkata were arrested near the bridge. They were carrying foreign arms and ammunition. It seemed that they had come to murder Ranababu. The news reached the S.P. who was extremely anxious about the MLA's safety and security. Ranababu used to cross the bridge to go to the school campus. The boys were flogged but the officer failed to extract any information from them. That night Tapobabu could not close his eyes even for a moment. He stood by the window looking at the night sky, thinking and reflecting.

The next morning, before Nidhu could report for duty, Tapobabu sent a message for him. He looked at Nidhu and wanted to know if Nidhu liked his animal-like existence.

Nidhu himself did not know what his life was like. To him, being alive meant certain specific factors like enjoying a square meal every day, reporting for duty twice a day, a litre of homemade rice beer, and a dhoti or a pair of khaki trousers. That was all. This was how his dawn gave way to day, the day to evening, and the evening to night.

Time was fleeting. The two policemen looking to make easy money were on the main road stopping trucks. The chowkidar brought tea. Nidhu finished it in no time and offered the chowkidar a *bidi*. The constable had gone for lunch. The others sat waiting for the police jeep and the van that would take the corpse away. Nidhu felt hungry at this hour of the afternoon. He had come in a hurry. Wherever he looked, he saw rice—near, far, by the side of the river, near the bamboo clumps the thick, wild kind; all he could think of was rice. A dove cooed from a treetop and the blue overarching dome above seemed to be smiling at them. Nidhu felt very sad for Tapobabu. He felt sad for anybody who played with fire and its fury. Once while looking for a cigarette, Nidhu had found a weapon wrapped in black cloth under the pillow in Tapobabu's room. He had trembled in fear and anxiety. He wondered whether Tapobabu had any link with those people from Kolkata. Everything had been puzzling and his heart had begun beating fast. He had often seen a similar weapon hanging from the officer's belt. The officer had killed two persons with that only a month ago. Late at night when Nidhu had been busy removing the dead bodies, he had been told that the two were seen playing at the crossing of the four roads with Nikunja Doctor's skull and they had been caught. The very next day, a group of unidentified youths had snatched away Samantababu's rifle from him at the police station and about twenty-five thousand rupees from Naran Muktar. That night, Tapobabu had come to Dompara. Nidhu was amazed. It was not usual for the people of the high castes to frequent their area where only members of the lower caste lived. Tapobabu, of course, did not believe in divisions based on caste and creed.

He had woken Nidhu up and thrust the weapon into his hands, saying, "Keep this. If you lose it, our group might be in trouble." Nidhu couldn't say no. He sat there with the weapon in his hand, trying to understand Tapobabu's motives. Finally, he had pushed it far inside the haystack. He couldn't sleep after that. Since then, the weapon was with him. Many a time, Nidhu had thought of throwing it into the deep waters. But he couldn't. It seemed as if Tapobabu was standing there in front of him, telling him, "It's my life. And I am leaving it here with you." Nidhu's eyes ached. The weapon was now in the earthen pot in which rice was kept. The old lady was no more; he had to take care of his own cooking now. Every time he went to measure out rice, he saw the weapon. He felt as though he saw the second officer himself, and regained his strength and courage.

The police jeep arrived and the cattle were driven into the cowsheds. The chowkidar had shared his lunch with Nidhu in the afternoon. Nidhu felt sleepy now; it was after a long time that he ate rice with fish curry and fried brinjals. Still, he stayed up for fear of the constable. Receiving a signal from the jeep, the officer walked confidently towards the corpse. Along with him went Ranababu, the heart-throb of the village. Every day his name adorned the headlines of the newspapers. His lectures and views took Kolkata by storm. Even if the audience wished to go home, they couldn't; they were held back by the magic of Ranababu's speech. It was a god-given talent. At every meeting, the big boss would mention how in the past he had to pawn his wife's necklace to have enough money to fight the election.

Nidhu ran forward to meet him and to pay him respect. Ranababu dropped his cigarette and went towards the place where the swollen corpse lay uncovered. Tarini, the tea stall owner, rushed in with an application, reminding Ranababu that he had promised to get Tarini's wife admitted in a hospital at Kolkata. But before he could finish, the police pushed him away roughly. Nidhu too moved aside.

The officer was busy taking notes. He asked the police about the corpse. Seeing Nidhu, he asked, "Have you searched the body?" The police nodded their heads. The officer asked, "Where are the belongings?"

"Empty, sir. He was very clever, sir!"

"No good deed can be achieved by cleverness," the officer said philosophically, and added, "Cleverness will be the end of you."

The photographer took pictures of the corpse. Then the officer announced that it was to be moved to the district town that day as per the orders of the S.P.

Nidhu lifted the body and placed it gently in the van-rickshaw. Then he tied it firmly. The rickshaw raced along the narrow, winding road through the cluster of sal trees. The chowkidar also ran alongside with a fat stick in hand. They met Kartikbabu at the crossing. People said that he had lost his balance of mind. The van-rickshaw stopped. The generous morning sun had spread light far and wide. Kartikbabu came forward and said, "O Nidhu, my dear, remove the cover. Let me see his face."

Nidhu did accordingly. His heart went out to Kartikbabu who stood there in front of him. Wearing a dirty dhoti, a ragged shirt, torn slippers with straps held together by a safety pin, stood Kartikbabu, the reputed English teacher, now bent and broken.

Kartikbabu started trembling as Nidhu removed the white cover. He slumped down on the ground, lamenting that the last pole that had held him together had now been cruelly removed. If all the supports were removed one by one like this, wouldn't the house crumble? Nidhu couldn't speak. The hopeless pitiable father lit a bidi and said, "I feel Tapo is no more. Had he been alive, he would have surely come home at least once to see his ailing mother. I have sent so many telegrams."

Nidhu pulled the van-rickshaw to the main road. He stood staring at Tapobabu's father who walked away, wiping the sweat from his forehead. There was work to be done. He had to take the official papers from the police station. That meant spending the entire night on the van. The police would reach there at about ten the next morning. If he couldn't reach the district town before that, there would be trouble. The post-mortem would get delayed. So Nidhu did as things ought to be done in such situations. However, first he went to have a full meal. Then he went to the police station where he found the police playing cards and gambling away the time. Nidhu felt sleepy as he sat there. It would be a long time before the papers and the other formalities would be completed. The officer on duty wasn't free. So Nidhu decided to sleep, and then he dreamt a wonderful dream.

Tapobabu had returned. There was no pain, no suffering, no sorrow, no misfortune anywhere. A gentle wind blew, and birds circled over the green fields and sang sweet songs. The day was bright. Tapobabu heaved a sigh of relief on seeing Nidhu. He said, "Give me a cigarette. It's a happy day. We will sing and dance all night long."

But Nidhu could not light the cigarette. His hands were bleeding and the skin was peeling off and falling in bits. He screamed out in fear.

A policeman shook him awake. Nidhu sat up straight with a jerk. He went out and splashed cold water on his face. He didn't wait. He took the papers and walked on along the red graveled road through the cluster of sal trees to reach the main road. On reaching the main road, Nidhu became a different person. He raced on with the van-rickshaw.

The sky darkened as night fell. The moon smiled down upon them as stars peeped out one by one. White clouds gathered in one corner of the sky watching their reflection in the waters of the Ganga. After crossing the overbridge, Nidhu stopped. He thought about the road he had just left behind.

The main hospital was only four miles from this village. He had crossed this road so many times. But never had he observed the Ganga so closely. Tapobabu used to say that the Ganga was for all. Nidhu Dom pushed two large pieces of gravel under the wheels of the van-rickshaw and started singing. The sober light of the radiant moon flooded the landscape. Nidhu forgot his surroundings, his duty. He remembered that he still had Tapobabu's weapon with him. Where, oh, where was Tapobabu? The man lying on the van had a striking resemblance with Tapobabu. Nidhu looked at the body and his heart filled with sorrow. The doctors would soon dissect this beautiful body. It would then be covered with red blood which would clot and look so hideous. Then the body would be handed back to him. The van, the sheets, the rope—everything would be soaked in blood.

"Why did you come? Why, Babu?" Nidhu pressed his palms against his temples. Tapobabu was there in front of him, smiling. "Nidhu Khuro, one day you will have enough to eat. Nobody will exploit you. Our fight is against the rich who exploit men like you and your class."

Nidhu walked towards the van trembling. He had committed many sins in his life. What was the harm if he did something good and worthwhile for once, only to become better by the touch of a good man? Nidhu untied the knots one by one. He hauled the corpse and walked slowly, step by step, towards the path that would take him to the riverbed. He forgot all about his duty and the consequences of his actions as he stepped on the white sand.

Nidhu remembered the abject misery and humiliation his father had been subjected to. What is the use of such a life where they were desecrated and deprived of their basic rights? The thought filled him with pity and despair. The vast stretches of the riverbed gave him strength and courage.

He bent down for one last time to place the body on the floating stream that would carry it far away beyond the limits of time and space. Then, the thin man, who was always bent double in slave-like docility, stood up straight with his head held high for the first time in his life.

Translated by Anuradha Sen

THE SEEDS

Tuniya looked at the hot sun standing alone in the sky and shuddered in fear. Her fear and anxiety were shared by all in the village. There had been no rains for a whole month. The village blazed under a hot tin sky. The scorched land was covered with thorny plants. The land—singed and brown and barren—robbed the villagers of their peace of mind. Only the tall trees stood, and even they seemed to be lifeless. One could tell they were still alive by the faint rustle of the near-brown leaves that clung on to the branches in desperation.

Tuniya had gone to the village pond in the afternoon. She came back with tears in her eyes. Gomiya, her husband, looked up at her as she spoke. "The water that used to be clear is now turbid. There is no sign of life anywhere. The mud sticks to you if you try to take a dip. Ugh! If this continues, even this water will dry up within forty-eight hours." She paused, and then continued, "What will we do then? Where will we take a bath? Where will we find water to drink and cook our meals?"

The whole village was in the grip of these fears. There was an acute scarcity of water. People had become restless. It was as hot as a forest fire. People were stripped of all positive emotions; the village folk no longer chatted or gossiped. They hardly spoke to each other these days. Gomiya tried to shake off the heavy sultriness of the summer and looked at his wife sadly. "If the gods wish to kill us, who can save us? The water level in the well is going down hour by hour. Soon the water will vanish into the bowels of the earth. If it does not rain, all we can do is cry."

Gomiya tilled the lands for cultivation. About one-fourth of an acre lay in front of their hut and the rest was by the riverside. If he did not work the whole year round, he and his family would starve to death. The lands kept them alive. Looking at Gomiya's pale and wan face, Tuniya's heart filled with sorrow. In a low voice she said, "I don't know what will happen. I feel so uncertain and hopeless these days. I think we are going to die."

"A *puja* has to be offered," said the Mukhiya, the village chief. Nobody protested. Every house paid the contribution grudgingly. Pujas were offered, and even an animal was sacrificed. Gomiya took the lead in the sacrificial ceremony. Then, as was the custom, he distributed the *prasad*. But all in vain. The fierce sun continued to rule the sky. It did not allow even a cloudlet to encroach on its kingdom. The breeze had lost its cool and refreshing touch. It only spread the harsh, hot breath of the sun.

Tuniya pushed a dry twig into the fire. Beads of sweat gathered on her forehead. She looked at her husband who was getting ready to go out. With fear in her eyes she said, "Where are you going in this fierce heat? There are heat waves sweeping across the land. The sun is blazing. Stay home. Go out after sundown." But nothing could stop Gomiya. He hated staying at home. He liked to work. If he didn't, he felt he would lose both his strength and his peace of mind.

Their youngest son Lallu had gone out to play. He came in running and said agitatedly, "Baba, come and see... there are cracks in the land. Bhai's feet got stuck in a crevice. His skin is badly flayed. He is limping. The land is wet with his blood."

The crevices had appeared nearly a month ago. Snakes and insects hid inside them. The other day, sheer luck had saved Gomiya from a snakebite. He had then pulled out the snake and killed it. His eyes spilled anger and hatred for the sun that made life so difficult. The heat waves had scorched everything and every relationship. At night when Tuniya had tried to draw him close to her, he had jerked her hands away in disgust and snarled in the darkness.

"Get lost! I have no energy left. Move to the corner. Until it rains, my mind will not calm down. Only a cool shower can soothe my agitation."

Disappointed, Tuniya had withdrawn into herself. Not once did she blame Gomiya. Rage and terror went hand in hand. She blamed the sun for it all.

It was a hilly area. Red dust flew all over the place. Tuniya went out in that brutal heat everyday to collect dried twigs and leaves for fire. She returned tired and worn out with a jackfruit and a wood apple. Her dark, sunburnt face did not excite Gomiya.

The Block Development Officer had come to their village about seven days ago. His jeep stood under the banyan tree. The suited and booted officer had spoken to them. He told them about the hybrid seeds that the Government would give the farmers. He was confident that the village folk would benefit and had urged them to enquire about it as soon as the rains set in. Everybody stood in shocked silence. The jeep had left leaving behind a cloud of dust. The Mukhiya had said in a serious tone, "Let it rain, then we shall see."

What good would it be to sow seeds in this stony soil, thought Gomiya. Tuniya longed for a daughter. Her desire made Gomiya restless. Mongru's daughter often came to their house. Tuniya would kiss her, caress her and put a bindi on her forehead. Then she would just sit there gazing at the little girl. This scene disturbed Gomiya. He had not breathed a word of his dream to Tuniya. He kept his wishes hidden.

After sundown the people got some respite. They flocked to the village well. They drew out water that accumulated at the bottom. With difficulty Tuniya too could fetch two full buckets of water. Drawing a bucket of water from such great depth was no joke. Even then she would always splash some cold water on her face. Its soothing coolness made the burning vanish like magic and calmed her. Her eyes lost their angry glare at moments like these. For a moment everything seemed to be so beautiful.

The people no longer spoke to the sky these days. The sky had become their enemy. The scorched land joined them in cursing the sky. Gomiya stood by the field lamenting and begging and praying for water, "Just a little water. We cannot live without it. O Marangburu, give us water." This was the prayer on everyone's lips. Their hearts broke as they looked up at the merciless sky.

The land became hotter. The wells dried up one by one. Crevices covered the land that was once lush green. Heat waves darted like poisonous arrows in all directions. Gomiya thought of the hard times that were in store for them as he drank rice beer. There was no solution. People simply had to get singed like the tall trees that could not save themselves from the sun. At times, a tired Tuniya would cry out, "I cannot endure it any more! It is too much! O Marangburu, please be merciful! Please help us." A small child cried out in pain. His mother gently pulled his feet out of the crevice. She incessantly abused and cursed the sky. "Why don't you die? Why should *we* die? Just staring at your spotless blue expanse will not help us. We need food. Our stomachs are crying out for food."

Gomiya had fallen asleep late at night after a long and tiring day. He dreamt of torrential rain. The brown land was covered with water. Tuniya stood in ankle-deep water and called out to him, "Didn't I tell you that it will rain? The sky protects us, it never kills." Tuniya looked beautiful. She looked as young and blithe as the green grass. Her supple body bubbled with life as she came running in the rain. The oxen stood under the *mahua* trees. Tuniya's passionate words reached him through the rain: "The sky has kept its promise. Now it is your turn."

Gomiya smiled. He could once again feel his blood surge with love. He touched the hand that he had pushed away in disgust one day. The rainwater filled up all the crevices. All around them the air was filled with the music of the rain. It had been so long since Gomiya had heard such wonderful music.

Tuniya woke Gomiya up. With sleepy eyes, he looked at his wife. Still in a daze of the lingering dream, he rebuked her mildly, "Why did you wake me? Why did you end the wonderful dream? I saw the sky overcast with thick black clouds. I saw torrential rain. Yet it was not dark. There was a faint light in the sky." He continued dreamily, "You were standing, getting drenched, and I was ploughing the land. O God, O Marangburu, if only it wasn't a dream!"

Tuniya's gentle eyes grew dreamy too. She said in a calm voice, "Even I was asleep. Suddenly I woke up and saw a black cloud sailing across the sky. I went out. And yes, it was just as I had seen a moment ago. Come, come outside. See how black and threatening the cloud is! Won't a cloud like this bring rain?"

Gomiya ran outside. Tuniya followed him. With eyes wide open he saw the pregnant cloud sailing across. For a fraction of a second he felt it was not a cloud but Tuniya herself. Overwhelmed with emotion, Gomiya turned around to look at his wife. He told her that his hopes and dreams will soon be fulfilled, "And then it will be your turn. But before that, I have work to complete."

Tuniya drew in a deep breath. She said, "No more sleep tonight. Come, let us go and wake everyone up. I love to convey good news." They hadn't gone far when it started drizzling. And then the rain came down in torrents. Tuniya sat down on the parched land, soaking in the water like the earth and getting drenched. Gomiya told her not to—she might fall sick. Didn't she know that she couldn't afford to fall sick now? Gomiya had his hands full: he would be tilling the land, sowing the seeds, tending the young plants.

Still Tuniya sat there. She wanted to cool her body that had endured the fierce heat for so many days. After sometime, she returned home. Changing into a dry saree but still shivering, she said to Gomiya, "Go to the BDO office tomorrow. The officer had said that they will give us seeds. If that is the case, we can save some money. We need to buy shirts for Lallu and his brother."

"Won't you buy a saree?" Tuniya smiled on hearing her husband's words. She said, "Whatever I have is enough. Give me the money, I will save it. When I am pregnant, I will buy and eat whatever I feel like."

Thus began a new day, a clear dawn. Memories of the trying days past vanished like a bad dream. Now was a time to dream, a time to share and care. Along with the village folk, Gomiya went to the BDO office the very next day. The Mukhiya did not like this. When the group led by Gomiya returned, they saw the Mukhiya waiting under the banyan tree where all meetings were held. Chiding them, he said, "Throw away the seeds. If you sow them, your land will be ruined. The seeds are *pardeshi*, they are foreign seeds. Think—would a pardeshi ever help us? Can you really hope to enjoy what grows from such seeds?"

Gomiya protested, "We don't agree. The government has given us these seeds. The land is ready. We will sow the seeds."

"You go ahead if you wish. But don't you dare take the others with you. You have no right to lead everyone to disaster."

Hearing the Mukhiya's stern voice and his comments on the seeds, the others drew nearer, their faces now lined with doubt. Taking stock of the situation, the Mukhiya continued, "What belongs to others can never be ours. Don't you know this simple truth? Tell me if I am wrong."

Everybody looked at the Mukhiya, their mouths gaping in awe. And the Mukhiya, encouraged by the first signs of victory, carried on.

"The earth is our mother. If we scatter foreign grains, our mother will be annoyed. All our labour will be for nothing. We will starve to death. So do not fall into the trap laid by the office-people. They know many tricks. They come to us only because they have a vested interest. They do not come for our benefit. Think for yourselves: when you beg for rice, they refuse. Then how is it so easy for them to give away a kilo of grain to every house?"

Old Samaru lowered the sack full of grain. Standing face to face with the Mukhiya, he said, "How do we know that you are speaking the truth? Can you prove that you are right?"

"Of course I can. Last year the office-babus had given this grain to everybody in my father-in-law's village. What was the result? Hard times followed! I have seen it with my own eyes: people eating grass and weeds instead of rice. An arable village known for its rich produce suffered due to the whims of the babus. They told me that the seeds brought forth grains that had no substance. Brothers, a non-native paddy cannot save the honour of our land. If you do not believe me, go and see the condition of that village with your own eyes."

Gomiya did not like how the situation was turning in the Mukhiya's favour. He said, "Grain is grain. How does it matter if it is native or foreign, *deshi* or pardeshi? Look how round it is. They told us that if we sow these seeds, the produce will be much more than usual. The rice will be slender and white. Not like what we produce—rough and coarse". To support his words, Gomiya split a few grains. He showed everybody the crushed seeds. The slender white grains stood out prominently like stars on his palm. "Look, such is the rice from this grain. Can this betray us?"

The Mukhiya wiped his forehead. Then he said, "Go, sow it in your patch of land. Just because you wish to die, you cannot take the others with you. I will not allow you to destroy the village." He raised his hands and announced *jihad* against Gomiya. Bewildered, Gomiya stood staring. Samaru kicked at the sack full of grains, "I will not use these seeds. I will not walk into this death trap. My youngest son would have been alive today had I not taken him to the hospital. It was all my fault. I should have believed the exorciser."

Gomiya protested, "That is not true. Your youngest son died of tetanus. Had you taken him to the hospital right away, the timely treatment could have saved his life. But no. You and your faith in sorcery and all that stuff! What good came of it? He held back your son for one and a half days, and finally when he couldn't cure him, he let you take him to the hospital. And now you dare to accuse the doctors?"

Samaru was silent. The Mukhiya spoke, "Tell me, how many are cured at the hospital? The medicines they prescribe are too expensive. We cannot afford the treatment."

"Such words don't suit you. You are the head of the village, the Mukhiya. It is your duty to lead us along the right path," said Gomiya in anger.

Mukhiya said in a tone of despair, "Forget it. We were speaking about the produce and the seeds. Those who wish to sow these seeds despite knowing everything, I will not stop them. Who am I to stop you? Isn't it sad—I can neither stop you, nor can I see you perish before my eyes. I consider the whole village as my family. Any loss to anybody is my loss. That is why I am telling you, if you do not have seeds, take them from my granary. My religion is to help others."

Old Samaru was the first to change sides. Others joined him to say 'yes'. Samaru heaved a sigh of relief having found support without any confrontation. Lighting a *bidi* he said, "I need ten kilos of the best seed. After the harvest, I will return all my dues with interest." The rest of the villagers joined Samaru in their demand for grains.

The Mukhiya, now jubilant, said eagerly, "Well, I will give it to you on one condition. For every ten kilos you take, you will give me five extra at the time of harvest. This is not interest. It is my right. Look, if I had sold the grain and put the amount in a fixed deposit fund, then the bank would have given me a much higher interest. But I cannot charge you such a high interest. After all, you are my fellow villagers. That is why you will give me only fifteen in total."

"What will we do with these then?" asked someone from the crowd.

"What can you do? Give it to Gomiya if you want," said the Mukhiya. "The summer days caused him so much harm. He and his family have suffered terribly. His eldest son has badly hurt his foot. Help him. He needs the money."

With fire in his eyes, Samaru said, "No! Never! We will throw it into the river, but we will not give it to him. He tried to lead us down the wrong path."

The Mukhiya stopped Samaru and then ordered the others to be quiet. "Why will you throw away the paddy seeds? Use them. It will not be wise to throw it all away. We are going through hard times."

"What if we became pardeshis?" said another. Everybody applauded him. Samaru too supported him, saying, "There is wisdom in his words."

The Mukhiya was lost in thought. Samaru's hair had greyed with age, but despite his years, he was no wiser. Mukhiya remembered the time when the doctor had prescribed some medicine for Samaru. It was a mixture in a bottle. The bottle had paper markings that duly indicated the prescribed dose. He was to take three doses every day. Each time, Samaru had torn off some of the paper and swallowed it with water. Then he had gone back to the doctor to follow up and to request him for something better so that he could get well soon. The doctor was baffled. On questioning him, he learnt that Samaru had taken only the paper marked with the stripes, and not the medicine.

It didn't prick the Mukhiya's conscience when he cheated these simpleminded people.

Gomiya felt his heart would break. If only one person in the crowd had stood by him, he would have taught the rest a lesson. Picking up the heavy sack, Gomiya went home. He placed the sack near Tuniya. When she opened it, her face lit up on seeing the round seeds. She came and sat beside Gomiya and said, "The babus gave you all this! The seeds are so beautiful, so golden. Where will we sow them?"

"On our land, where else? Paddy seeds grow on land, not high up in the sky!" he snapped at her.

Tuniya observed her husband closely. His irritation betrayed anxiety. She gave him a bowl of rice beer and said, "Take this. It will help you." Then she quietly asked him, "What is it? Why are you so worried? I don't like it."

Gomiya finished the rice beer in a single gulp. He wiped his face and looked at Tuniya. It was a soft, loving look. Although a mother of two, Tuniya still looked as radiant as a new bride. She returned his gaze, a question and an appeal in her eyes. Gomiya told her casually about the Mukhiya and his tactics, "We were returning home with the seeds. The Mukhiya stopped us near the banyan tree. He told us that the seeds would ruin us. It is a sin to touch pardeshi seeds, he said. That there would be a famine and many other things."

"Didn't you say anything?"

"I did, but nobody cared to listen. That old Samaru led the others away. Tuniya, they could not understand—the Mukhiya simply hoodwinked them. The truth is that his paddy seeds have been rotting for a year. If everybody listened to the office-babus, what will the Mukhiya do with all his sacks full of seeds? He needs to make profit. So he tricked them."

Tuniya was surprised. "What are you saying! And everybody believed his stories?"

"Yes, they did," said Gomiya. "See it is very easy to fool us. We have no education, no knowledge about the world outside the village—nothing. And until we overcome this lack, until we know better, there will be no change. We will continue to be cheated by the Mukhiyas and the others like him."

Tuniya agreed. "We must send our sons to school. The teacher does not come to the village school. Next time you go to the office, speak about it."

"What is the use? It is the Mukhiya's son who is the teacher."

Tuniya did not like his defeatist words. She flatly opposed him and said, "I don't agree with you. Those who give us seeds, those who enquire about us from time to time, they cannot be our enemies. They are *our* people. And we must speak to them about our troubles and our grievances."

The torrential rain washed away the heat and the fatigue. As was the custom, Gomiya offered pujas before sowing seeds. Urged on by his passion for his work, by his refusal to resign to bad luck and by his unshaken belief that ultimately he would succeed, Gomiya worked with a zeal. From dawn till late in the afternoon, he worked in his field—ploughing, watering the paddy shoots, and watching them grow with eager eyes. Soon, the land was covered with saplings. Tuniya, toiling in the fields alongside her husband, said, "Can't you get a field hand to help you? Very soon we will have to replant the paddy shoots in well-arranged lines."

"You are tired, aren't you?" Gomiya looked at his wife with concern. "This time, nobody will come to work in our fields. The Mukhiya has ordered them not to. We are outcasts now."

"Why? What is our fault?" Tuniya asked with tears in her eyes. She stood up briefly to straighten her back and rest a little, and then continued, "Anybody can take help from the government. Why should he be so angry?"

"The rich and the powerful are always like that. They have punished me severely for a small fault. Now I just want to complete the work without any trouble."

He worked as he spoke, and so did Tuniya. The young green shoots stood upright in waist-deep water. After two weeks, they would replant them in neat, straight lines. The paddy field would then be covered in green—the colour of growth and prosperity. They were confident that there was hope for them though the situation was adverse. This hope soothed them and gave them strength.

The sky, that had only a couple of months ago appeared so heartless, now seemed to shower love, affection and a sense of security the way only a mother can. The sweet rain had brought back to life what was nearly ravaged. It revived hope and spread a sweet music, the music of life. The ruined homes were once again revived by the magic touch of the many shades of green as nature smiled. There was happiness all around. But Tuniya was not happy. Her heart was filled with sorrow for Gomiya who loved people and their company. After a hard day's work, when he went over to his neighbours' for a chit-chat, nobody offered him rice beer or even spoke to him freely. "Is my husband so wicked? What is his fault?" No one answered her questions. She lived her days thinking of the happy future. If they reaped a good harvest, then they had nothing to worry about. Not for a year at least. Tuniya decided she would use the hay for roofing the hut. And if everything turned out well, she would sell the grains to buy a radio. She dearly wanted to lie on the mat listening to songs, with the radio balanced on her breast.

In summer, the dirt road would gradually lose its identity as it wound its way down to the riverside and then disappear altogether as it plunged into the river. In the rainy season, the path was nowhere in sight. In the swollen, gushing river the heads of the waves sparkled in the sun like a brightly-lit throne. Seated on this throne, one could dream of the good days to come. Tuniya had to cross the river to reach home. In her mind's eye, she could see her sons playing in front of their house. Crossing the river was no problem for Tuniya, it had become a habit. She swam across it quickly and skillfully, like a fish. Water dripped from her saree onto the earth enveloped by the gathering darkness of dusk. The songs of the birds returning home filled her with joy. It was time to relax, time to dream.

Late at night when Gomiya returned, the moon stood benignly watching the sky. So majestic was its aura that the clouds seemed to part respectfully to give way to the moon. Tuniya was tired of waiting. Her face flooded with relief when she saw Gomiya. As they sat down for their meal, Gomiya told Tuniya about his meeting with old Samaru. "Do you know what he said to me today, drunk though he was?" Tuniya looked up enquiringly. Struggling to overcome his emotions, Gomiya said, "Samaru said that the pardeshi seeds will ruin us. That we will have to repent very soon. And there will be no way then to recover from the loss."

"What did you tell him?"

"What could I say? I said seeds grow in soil. What have seeds got to do with caste and creed? But he burst out laughing and said, 'All paddy seeds bring forth rice, but the qualities are different. That slender white rice of yours will not come in handy for making rice beer. You will always feel hungry.'" Gomiya paused, lost in thought. Then he said, "I told Samaru that whatever happens, I will see it through to the very end. But I just could not make him understand why."

"How will you wake up those who sleep with their eyes open?" said Tuniya thoughtfully. Looking at her, Gomiya said, "Yes. Until the people wake up by themselves, things will be difficult. The river does not have a dam. I have told the Mukhiya so many times to go to the MLA Sahib with a petition. But he did not listen to me. Nobody cared to listen. And so, every year in the rainy season, we face trouble. The people of one village cannot go to another village even in times of dire need."

"They are scared," said Tuniya. "They want everybody to remain illiterate and ignorant. Because then they can continue to dominate and exploit everyone. They can treat the whole lot like slaves. But this cannot go on. Those who have risen from their slumber will not bow down again."

"Your words give me strength. You are my hope, my inspiration. If you are with me, I have no fear."

Autumn arrived carrying with it a cool breeze. The catkin bushes were covered with flowers. The swollen river seemed frightful; Tuniya felt scared even to touch the water. The other day, her head had begun to reel. Gomiya soon understood the reason. Surprised, he asked her, "Why don't you eat?"

"I feel nauseous, I cannot eat anything." Tuniya's face flushed with happiness and embarrassment. "How will I work in the fields?"

Gomiya smiled and reassured his wife that he wasn't dead yet. Overwhelmed with emotion, Tuniya said, "Wait and see, Goddess Lakshmi will come to our house this time."

Harvest time drew near. The peasants went only to their fields and farmyards now. Gomiya too did the same. He was so happy. His eyes lit up and his whole being radiated his joy—joy as pure as the vast expanse of clear blue that merged into the horizon. The produce this year was unexpected. In the first light of dawn, he looked at the green fields, spellbound at their glory and splendour. Dewdrops sparkled in the soft golden light. Gomiya decided that he would now concentrate on reaping. Tuniya's presence in the field would have been of immense help at this time. But how could he ask? It would be difficult for her to cross the river at this stage.

Tuniya, however, refused to listen. "I will go," she said stubbornly. "I was with you at the time of sowing. And I will be with you at the time of reaping."

"At that time, you were not carrying anyone within you. Now you should take rest. Let us not invite any misfortune. The roads are slippery. If anything happens, what will I do?" said Gomiya.

As the time for reaping drew closer, flocks of parrots flew in from the distant jungles. The whole day they circled over the field and ate the grains. To Gomiya it seemed that the parrots were the Mukhiya's representatives. One day he killed one and brought it home. Tuniya was scared. "What have you done! Why have you done this? The paddy does not belong to you alone. Unless the birds eat it, the paddy does not ripen."

The same night, Tuniya dreamt of the green parrots that flew in from the faraway jungles. Flapping their wings, they dived into the field, their faces marked with sorrow at having lost a friend the previous day. Their red beaks seemed redder and eager for revenge. They cut the crop with their sharp beaks and carried it away. The field was emptied of its treasure.

Tuniya cried out in her sleep. Gomiya tried to console her. "Don't cry," he said. "Everything was fine just yesterday. I saw with my own eyes the slender stalks swaying with the gentle breeze. I felt their excitement and marveled at their joyful sway. This year the produce from my field has put to shame all the others.""

"That is why I am so scared."

"Why are you scared? The office-babus have noted my name. They will give me a prize."

Someone carried this news to the Mukhiya. He was mad with anger. He said, "I will see how he gets the prize." Along with his supporters, he planned to take Gomiya down. He told them that Gomiya had gone against the tradition of the village. Because of him, they could not hold their heads high. So he must be punished. "I will see to it that he is totally destroyed," the Mukhiya declared.

"We should have uprooted the saplings then itself. Now it is too late. The village people will not spare you. They will tell the BDO everything. The times are not favourable, father," warned Kunkal, the Mukhiya's son.

Mukhiya looked at his son in fear. Then he said in a low voice, "Old Samaru is an expert in such matters. Go, bring him here. I will explain everything to him. He harbours a grudge against Gomiya. I only have to instigate him."

It was quite late when Kunkal returned with old Samaru. The Mukhiya was restlessly pacing to and fro. His eyes were red. Having had too many drinks, he found it difficult to speak clearly and coherently. His garbled words filled Samaru with fear. Still, he said, "I will not be disloyal to my benefactor after having eaten his salt. I will take up the stick for him."

"Then let us go right now."

As they were leaving, Samaru turned around to see the Mukhiya—he was about to lose his balance and fall. But who could stop him? They went out together. The Mukhiya ordered Samaru to go and call Gomiya, "I will wait behind the bush. Then together we will do the job. When everything is done, I will give you one-third of an acre. I will put it down in writing."

"One-third? That will keep me fed for the rest of my life. Good. Very good, babu!"

The Mukhiya was stumbling along with difficulty. His head reeled and he saw stars. His throat felt impossibly parched. Then, unable to walk any further, he stopped and asked Samaru for water.

"Water! Where will I get water from now? There is a well nearby but how will I draw water without a bucket?"

"Then?"

"There is a way. Let us take the road that runs along the river. It is quite close by. Listen carefully—you can hear the sounds of the flowing water."

"Then take me there. I need water. I cannot walk."

Samaru led the Mukhiya in the darkness of the night. He was thinking of Gomiya. How bold and determined he was! How he bravely stood against the village all alone. He fought against them all. Samaru thought of what Gomiya had told him, "How can paddy seeds be deshi or pardeshi? Wherever there is land, there grows paddy. Do you believe otherwise? Our paddy seeds yield less produce. The office-babus brought these seeds for us, for our benefit, and yet you did not believe them. You mistook gold for brass. This hurt me the most. How could you be so unreasonable, Khuro?"

Samaru could now see for himself and understand how right Gomiya was every time he passed the fields. Now that he understood the dirty trick the Mukhiya had played on them, Samaru could no longer stand him. When the Mukhiya and his henchmen wanted to destroy Gomiya's saplings, Samaru had stopped them. He had said, "You cannot stop him this way. Next year, he will do the same thing again. So it is not the harvest that we should remove but the man himself. He is as much my enemy as yours. We must kill him. Let me do it." But these words were only a means to save the crop. For Samaru, Gomiya's crop was like his own child. He had already lost his youngest son. He did not wish to make the same mistake twice.

They had reached the riverside. The Mukhiya kept on saying, "Water! Water! I am so thirsty. I see water everywhere but I feel I will not be able to quench my thirst."

Samaru laughed. "Thirst is ever-growing, babu. It is unquenchable. Like yours."

They were very close to the water. There was pitch darkness all around. Only fireflies blinked to show the way. The river hissed like a serpent.

The Mukhiya started drinking water. Samaru stood behind him, dreaming of Gomiya's lush rice fields. He was so old but never had he seen such beautiful golden rice fields before! Yes, Gomiya truly had God Marangburu's blessings! Watching the Mukhiya drink, Samaru felt as if the man was a wild beast, a tiger that had emerged from the nearby jungles. It would quench its thirst and then enter the village to kill people.

Their village had only one real man. Samaru would not allow the tiger to kill him. A human being could never be on friendly terms with a tiger which would demand human blood and flesh everyday. To make the difficult job easier, Samaru did not waste any more time. His eyes lit up as he kicked the Mukhiya forcefully from behind. Like a felled tree the man toppled into the dark roiling waters. He tried to swim but could not. The current swiftly carried him along.

There was no cry of pain. Samaru laughed as the sound of the waves reached him. His laughter rippled across the swelling river and onto the rice fields and beyond, from one field to another.

Translated by Anuradha Sen

URANGARA

Urangara is a tributary of the river Subarnarekha.

Snehamoy had not been to the river in nearly a year. Ever since Sayantani arrived, time had flowed sluggishly, lazily, like the waters of the Subarnarekha. No work had been done. Only a year back, he had a deep and intense attachment to the river. So often in the past Snehamoy had walked by the river in the evening as the light of the setting sun fell on the water and the mountains. The calm and gentle wind stirred his mind and his desire to settle down.

The railway bridge shook violently as the train speeded along. The friendly murmur of the river became a loud gurgling sound. The earth trembled, the jungles shuddered and the timid rabbit ran to its shelter. Snehamoy watched all this. He simply watched.

Nobody would ever know how quickly nature can change its colours and hues unless they came to the riverbank. Sitting by the river, he could see at dawn the waters turning into gold and the dazzling red of the sun changing to a warm pink like the buds that bloom on the serene edge of a forest stream. Later in the day, the water would turn a sober shade of silver and blue, like the veil of mist that covers faraway mountains, briefly.

Muri was neither a town nor a village. The sound of the water flowing over the smooth pebbles, a sweet babble, would reach Snehamoy even as the loud, piercing, sound of the shunting steam engine disturbed the quiet of this small railway station. A little away from the Subarnarekha was the forest with *palash* and *shimul* trees. The riverbanks glowed bright with the beautiful wild red flowers that attracted the bees and the birds that glided among the trees. The strong currents carried the flowers to unknown distant lands. The Adibasi girls would often pick them up and pin them to their tight buns. Their dry, unkempt and dishevelled hair looked so beautiful with the red flowers, so unprofitably gay.

Sayantani had arrived from Kolkata. She dressed up beautifully in the evenings. She loved to dress up, and had brought with her everything she needed for her make-up and outfits. When Snehamoy returned home from office in the evening, he forgot about the Subarnarekha completely. In front of him was another river, gentle and flowing, in all its glory. It kept Snehamoy spellbound. He could not take his eyes off her and the sensual curves of her beautiful body, youthful and lively. He said, "Why should I go to the riverside when a river flows in my own house?"

Sayantani's expression changed. A frown appeared on her beautiful smiling face and she said, "You always avoid going there. This Sunday I will not listen to any excuses. I will go."

Soon it was Sunday.

Snehamoy felt restless. He opened all the windows one by one and looked towards Muri Tungri. Even with all the windows open, sunlight did not enter the rooms. There was always a soft shadow that played about in the room. With Sayantani around, time flew. How swiftly the hours passed when he was with her! Both of them were amazed as Snehamoy opened the windows: dusk had set in. The swishing of the gentle wind and the soft gurgle of the river reached them. They were charmed by the loveliness, by the sense of mystery that the darkness evoked. Yet Sayantani said childishly, "Oh no! How will we go? Soon it will be night." Snehamoy replied, "Some other day, not today". But Sayantani insisted, "No. Today itself. You have to keep your word." Snehamoy was surprised at Sayantani's eagerness. It seemed to him that she was Urangara, the tributary, who was eager and impatient to join the Subarnarekha. "Will you tell me why you are so eager to see the river? Have you never seen a river before?"

"Yes, I have," Sayantani replied, "But only the Ganges. I have seen it a number of times while going to Kalighat and Belur."

"And yet you are not satisfied."

Snehamoy's words hurt her. Her excitement vanished and she was quiet for a while. Then she said, "The Ganges is a calm river. It is not wild and exciting like the Subarnarekha. Bhakua told me about how turbulent it becomes in the rains and how it swells. Last monsoon, it had become a rushing torrent and swept away bushes and small trees. It carried off the cattle. It caused such havoc."

"Bhakua told you all this?" Snehamoy said.

"Yes. I pass my time chatting with him since you are busy at office. Bhakua said that Subarnarekha is a *rakshasi*—ferocious and monstrous, and malevolent too. Every year she demands a head."

"Bhakua tells such tales."

Sayantani did not agree. Walking away, she said, "He will not tell me lies. The Adibasis are very honest and simple people. And he is quite old. Why would he lie?"

Snehamoy lit a cigarette. He was annoyed with Bhakua. That old man had nothing better to do. Ever since she had offered him a cup of tea, he called Sayantani 'Maiji'. A broad-shouldered and hefty man, his thickset eyebrows and foggy eyes evoked fear in people. One day he had shown Snehamoy a deep, ugly wound on his back, which had frightened Snehamoy. When he asked,

"What happened?" Bhakua had casually said it was nothing. A bear had attacked him. Its sharp claws had dug out his flesh. Had he not been carrying his axe with him, he would have been dead. A bear had the strength of several buffaloes—how could a man fight it alone?

Bhakua used to go to the forest to cut trees for wood. That was his profession. If the forest guards were there, Bhakua would move about as stealthily and cautiously as the leopard. He swung his axe with a sure aim; his old, sinewy arms did not yet tremble. A seer of rice beer was enough for Bhakua. When he drank rice beer, he felt like a nawab, the king of the jungle. He cared for no one and he spoke what came to his mind. His abusive language and filthy words unsettled people and made them uneasy. Bhakua had once told Snehamoy that everything belonged to him. The forest, the river, the land, the sky—it all belonged to Bhakua, the Adibasi, and yet he had nothing to eat. No one gave him dry chapatis even. They were all ungrateful, all selfish opportunists, he said. Pointing a finger at himself, Bhakua said that his body had no more strength left and it would crumble like an anthill one day. He would starve to death along with his daughter, for he had no work and no money.

Snehamoy was surprised. When the man spoke in a loud voice and beat upon his chest with his fist, it sounded like the roar of the Niagara. His throat produced a harsh, grating sound and drops of sweat stood out on his wrinkled forehead.

Snehamoy had first made the acquaintance of Bhakua in his flat. The man had one day presented himself, with a pole resting on his shoulder from the ends of which hung two large, heavy bales of firewood and a wounded wild hen. Snehamoy had taken him to be a thief and had been immediately on his guard. Bhakua, unaware of how Snehamoy perceived him, had said, "Babu, I have not eaten anything for two days. I am not well. My daughter is starving. Take the firewood. I will give it for cheap." Snehamoy had no need for firewood. Yet, seeing the pitiable condition of the old man, he had bought it. His generosity had surprised Bhakua, who had with folded hands said, "God will be good to you. The man who cares for the poor and the downtrodden, Singbonga cares for him." Then he had gifted the wild hen to Snehamoy, his face flooding with delight as he coaxed him, "Take it, Babu. You will like the taste. Don't you see the shine on the feathers?"

Snehamoy had wanted to pay him for the bird but Bhakua had refused outright. Shaking his head vehemently, he had said, "No, I will not take it. It will be a sin if I do."

Since then, Bhakua had been a regular visitor to his house. He was very fond of tea and if he was offered a cupful, he would light his *chutta*, stretch out his legs and dirty feet on the clean floor, and start chatting. The strong smell of tobacco smoke filled the room and Snehamoy felt intoxicated. But Bhakua drew in the smoke with ease and chatted merrily about his kinfolk—God knows how much rice beer he had drunk! His eyes lit up when he spoke about 'Karma Puja', and he proceeded to give Snehamoy, who had no clue about it, a detailed description of the puja in his hoarse voice. He described how they cut a branch of the *karam* tree and planted it firmly in the courtyard as a ritual. As he spoke he grew serious and his tone became solemn. They would plant the branch in the rice fields in the month of Bhadra. They believed that its divine power helped the paddy to sprout. In time, the fields would be covered with lush green stalks that swayed to and fro in the breeze, as graceful as girls when they reached adolescence. The Karma Puja was for blacksmiths and carpenters too. If the rituals were not performed according to the norms, then everything would dry up. There would be famine.

Snehamoy had seen Bhakua's poor hut. He had been astonished and wondered how a family of two could possibly stay in such a small space! Seeing him standing there, Bhakua had come splashing across the knee-deep water to greet him from the other side of the river, getting his dirty clothes completely wet. With a broad grin he had offered Snehamoy a chutta and said, "Take it, Babu, take my chutta today. I hand-rolled it myself. Inhale the smoke and enjoy the fun, the intoxication." Then he had pointed to a girl standing close by and said, "That is my daughter, Budni. Colder than the cold water of the well. Her mother is dead. She died seven years ago, of dysentery and vomiting. My wife could not enjoy any happiness in her lifetime. I want to see my daughter happy, that is all."

Snehamoy understood the deep bond between the father and the daughter. It was the same strong love that bound the rocks with the mountain, the river with the water, and the soil with roots. It was the same eternal love and affection that made Bhakua, the father, guard Budni.

Bhakua would not allow Snehamoy to leave. He had dragged Snehamoy to his hut. Budni had run away in embarrassment. Snehamoy had been stunned by the softness of her face—it did not glow unduly bright like glaring daylight but softly like the subtle light of the stars. Snehamoy had kept staring in wonder.

Budni was a grown-up girl, almost an adult. The darkness of her complexion complemented the brightness of her eyes and made her look even more beautiful and attractive. To Snehamoy, she seemed to be the queen of this hilly town. Bhakua ordered her brusquely, "Budni, ey Budni. Bring some rice beer for Babusahib." She came with a bowl, crooked and bent, which contained the cloudy white drink. The saree wrapped around her body only enhanced her graceful curves. Snehamoy's heart skipped a beat as he caught a glimpse of her ample bosom. "Beautiful!" he whispered.

Bhakua said to him, "Ey Babu, I beg of you, please give Budni some work. Any odd job will do. Sorrow and misfortune have accompanied my daughter right from her birth. I cannot provide her even a square meal, the wretched man that I am. If I die without righting this wrong, the vultures will tear me to pieces for my sin. Save me, Babu."

Snehamoy had come away that day with great difficulty. But only seven days later, Bhakua had come to his flat along with Budni. With folded hands he had said, "I have brought my daughter. She is your responsibility from now on. I give her to you." Snehamoy had been confounded to hear Bhakua's words. Budni was standing silently near the door. Seeing her face clouded with fear and sorrow, Snehamoy had felt sad. Bhakua had scolded his daughter, "Why are you standing there? Don't you know that you should touch his feet? He is not a man, he is our God."

Budni had done as she was told. Bhakua had seemed very happy and proud to see his daughter's humble manners. He had said, "Babu, ey Babu, say something. My daughter is an expert. Give her any kind of work. If not at the office, at least here in your house. She will cook your meals, wash the utensils ... Just give her twenty-five rupees at the end of the month."

Sayantani came into the room humming a tune. Snehamoy's thoughts scattered as he turned and looked at her. Girls look beautiful when they come out after a bath, he thought. Sayantani was pretty but now she appeared all the more beautiful, like a water nymph with drops of water that dripped from her long black hair onto her smooth skin. Sayantani requested him to bring her the moss-green saree that she wanted to wear. Bhakua had told her that the water of the Subarnarekha was green in colour. Surely the saree would match with it! Snehamoy felt shy, but he went ahead and gave her the saree. Wrapping the silk saree around her still-wet body, Sayantani laughed. She said, "Hey! Do I look like the river?" She struck a dancer's pose. Her movements were fluid, graceful and sensual. Snehamoy was captivated. Entranced. Looking at her beautiful body, he felt as if she was a river in a woman's guise.

The next moment he realised his mistake as he remembered Budni's words. Pointing towards the Urangara, she had said, "Babu, this is only a tributary; there are so many twists and turns.

But it has nothing—no ebb, no flow. No matter how much you jump and splash around in it or crush its heart, it will not drown you. It will endure everything. Like us. Like me."

If Sayantani was Subarnarekha, then Budni was Urangara. There was a flow in both, but they were like two different kinds of snake. If one was deadly, the other was harmless and easy-going. Both had slippery bodies and fangs, but their poisons were different. The bite of one brought instantaneous death, while the other one intoxicated. Sayantani's slick, curvaceous body slithered like the deadly snake, its hiss the loud, roaring music that he heard every time he stood by the Subarnarekha where the water crashed against the stones and pebbles in the golden sand and kissed the riverbank. But the melody of the Urangara was sweeter than that of the flute. The curves of Budni's bosom were like the waves of the Urangara. To be able to hear that sweet sound, one would have to surrender one's name, one's self and pride, forget the world, and listen with his ears against her soft breasts.

Sayantani came closer. The fragrance of the *kunda* flower woke Snehamoy from his reverie. He said, "This fragrance... I know it so well—it is your fragrance." Sayantani was not surprised. She smiled and said, "It is not mine. It is the body soap. Yes, I too like it."

It seemed to Snehamoy that the point where the Urangara and Subarnarekha met, the same fragrance wafted about in the air. The fragrance of a person and a river must be alike then.

Budni had come in the afternoon. It was a hot day and she was sweating profusely. She said, "Please give me ten rupees. I will give it back. Babuji is not well. He fell down from the tree. He is badly hurt. I have to buy medicines." She was covered in sweat and dust and looked exhausted. She said, "Babu, please give me a glass of water. The whole day I have been collecting coal. Still the bag is not full. Only one full bag will fetch me five rupees."

Snehamoy realised that Budni was hungry. She had not eaten anything, while only an hour ago he'd had rice and mutton. The couple of months that Budni had worked for him, Snehamoy had no trouble, and neither did Budni. She ate as much as she liked. Snehamoy would often reassure her that she could eat her fill, and that he would not become poor if she ate as much as she wanted to.

The comfort and food brought had about a visible change in her appearance. There was a tint in her cheeks and her dark forehead glowed, which added to her beauty. Snehamoy could not take his eyes off her. He did not know whether Budni understood his feelings. Yet, whenever he looked at the poor girl with love-sick eyes, he imagined Sayantani glaring at him. The letters that came from Calcutta gave rise to a deep longing in Snehamoy that disturbed him terribly. Strange thoughts came to his head and he could see Sayantani, the living, breathing Sayantani, his beloved Sayantani in front of him.

Sayantani's letters, her strong presence in her absence, created a wall between Snehamoy and Budni. He could not break down that wall. His education, his job, his reputation, his status—everything was against him. He desired Budni. He imagined himself as her lover. But this was as far as he could go. He knew Sayantani would eventually come there, to his flat, as his duly married wife, clad in a Benarasi saree with a streak of vermillion in the parting of her hair. Who was Budni in comparison? An illiterate, uncultured girl, without any status in society, one who had nothing to eat.

Snehamoy gave Budni ten rupees and told her to take some rest and to eat before doing anything else. He was a communist at heart. He believed in socialism. He had neither turned her away nor fired her. But troubled by the snide remarks of the people of the neighbourhood, Budni had herself left. Bhakua had taken his daughter home. As he left, he had said as if in apology, "Babu, Budni will not come to work from tomorrow.

The people here are not nice, they say bad things. I feel angry. It will make it difficult for Budni to get married."

Snehamoy had said nothing. He had watched them leave in silence.

Since then, Budni had not visited this part of the railway colony. He was told that she went to the railway yard to buy coal. She would give the driver a rupee pinned to a long pole and he would drop a basket full of coal on the railway tracks. She sold the coal and the money it earned fed the father and daughter. If it really was enough, then why was Budni in this condition? Gone was her healthy glow; now she looked like a skeleton. The Urangara did not dry up so soon, not in the month of Phagun—it still had a flow, a forceful current.

After she had eaten, Budni went to the bathroom to wash and clean the utensils. She turned around to look at Snehamoy and said, "Bapu is right. You are God. There is still God among human beings." Then, as she opened the tap, water flowed on with full force and flooded the bathroom. Confused, Budni called out, "Babu, o Babu!"

Snehamoy ran in. Budni was completely drenched. She was trying hard to close the tap and stop the flow of water. In the process, the end of her saree had slipped off her shoulder, revealing her breasts. Snehamoy stood there looking at her for moments, until unable to control himself any longer he pulled her close and crushed her to his chest. He carried her light body and placed her upon the bed. The wild tiger raged about in the waters of Urangara for a long time. The river, born to dedicate itself to others, was calm.

Budni wiped her tears and looked at Snehamoy with brimming eyes. "I never thought that I would have to pay this price for a handful of rice, Babu. Had I known, I would never have stepped into the den as long as there was breath in this body." Budni's words pierced Snehamoy like a spear. Looking at Sayantani's letters, he was filled with remorse. Budni was crying, "Is this the act of a god? Where will I go with this sinful body now? The river is dry. I cannot even drown myself and die." Finally, on Snehamoy's urging, she wiped her tears and took a bath. Her body was scented with the fragrance of kunda flowers. Before leaving, she said, "Do not feel sad, Babu. And do not blame yourself alone. The river does not send back one who comes to it." Before leaving, Budni took the bar of scented soap and said, "I will get married on the fifteenth day of Phagun. On that day, I will use this soap again."

The road to the river was uneven. So he avoided it and took the shortcut. His slippers slipped off his feet every now and then. Yet Sayantani seemed to be walking along happily. As they turned around a bend, she suddenly clapped her hands like a child and shouted, "Come and see—oh just look at those daffodils! I think Wordsworth wrote that poem after seeing these flowers."

Snehamoy stopped. He said, "These are not daffodils. These are *putush* flowers. Their fragrance brings in flies and mosquitoes. And then the mosquito bites cause malaria." Sayantani hopped out from the spot and said, "What a beautiful sight! This could be a tourist spot." Snehamoy said nothing. There was no end to Sayantani's curiosity. The next moment, she said, "Can we get gold from the waters of Subarnarekha? Bhakua said that there was gold dust in the sand. Is there really?"

"Maybe..."

"Then I am definitely going to collect some. I will not leave without it."

Sayantani resembled a young girl without a care in the world, talking and laughing. After a while she said, "Listen, Bhakua told me there are poisonous snakes in the river. What should we do? I am not carrying a torch." Snehamoy was visibly irritated now. He said, "Will you stop this Bhakua-said-this, Bhakua-said-that business? When did he come? As far as I know he is admitted in the hospital. He has TB."

Sayantani said between pauses for breath, "He had come about six or seven months ago. It was then that he had told me all this." They were climbing a slope. A shower of pebbles came rattling down as she continued, "What a simple and honest man he is. And he can narrate stories so beautifully! He looks so much like the old man in *The Old Man and the Sea*."

Tuberculosis was a curable disease, but Snehamoy knew that Bhakua would not survive. To the Adibasi it was a grave affliction. And rice beer was neither the medicine nor the diet for the sick, yet Bhakua drank it, trying to drown his sorrows in alcohol.

Sayantani stood by the river, looking at the setting sun; its pale crimson light had flooded the landscape. Then like an obstinate child, she walked on, determined to cross the river and to walk on the sand.

"This side has only stones and gravel," she said.

"You will spoil your saree!"

"It doesn't matter, come on."

Together, they crossed the river to go to the other side. Snehamoy remembered the day he had gone there to survey the area. Budni had been on the other side, wearing a bright yellow printed saree and a necklace of yellow beads. She had met him. Putting down the bundle she had been carrying, she had bent down to touch his feet. She had said, "I am getting married on the fifteenth day of Phagun. You have to come. I will make rice beer myself on that day. We will sing and dance. You too must dance with us."

Snehamoy had looked at Budni in surprise mingled with respect. This poor illiterate girl had forgiven him so soon. From where did these people learn such generosity of spirit, such simplicity and humility? How did they defeat with such ease the proud, arrogant people from big cities? Snehamoy had not been able to look up and meet her gaze. He had only said, "I will come. I will surely come. It will be a great sin on my part if I don't."

Sayantani came up to him, smiling. Snehamoy said, "You are not afraid, are you? Do you know there are invisible currents in this river?" Sayantani laughed and said, "Our life is full of invisible currents. At any moment we may be carried away or we may drown—who knows what will happen? So I don't think much about it."

The Urangara flowed on by the Kathari mountain to ultimately converge with the waters of the Subarnarekha. In complete self-sacrifice, she surrendered her smaller, independent identity to merge with the larger river. But then, who would not want to transcend one's limits to reach magnificence?

Sayantani asked him the name of the tributary.

"Urangara."

"Beautiful. Very uncommon. How many such tributaries are there?"

Snehamoy told her that the Urangara flowed on unseen, unnoticed. Nobody knew where and no one cared.

They had reached the forest. The large stretch of golden sand welcomed those who cared to lie down and rest.

Sayantani sat down on the sandy beach to search for gold dust. If she found even a single grain—then what next? Perhaps this is how people ran after gold, Snehamoy thought. She called out to him, "Keep searching, we will find it. We will not fail like the rest." Snehamoy did not like the idea. "It is nothing but a rumour," he said. They walked about on the sands together for a while. Then it was time to return. Disappointed, Sayantani said, "I never thought that the Subarnarekha would fool us."

The electric lights of the station could be seen from a distance. When they were crossing the slope and were close to the railway colony, they saw a young Adibasi girl carrying a bundle of firewood on her head. In the half-light of the falling dusk, her face could not be seen clearly. She was wearing a thin, torn saree that barely covered her body. Tied to her back and held in a cloth sling, a baby, perhaps five months old, was sleeping peacefully.

The girl crossed the forest and stood face-to-face with them. Putting down the bundle of firewood, she called out in joy, "Babu, ey Babu!"

Snehamoy was taken aback. "Budni!"

"Ho, Babu!"

"When did you come back from your husband's house?"

"A long time, Babu. It has been nearly six months now."

"Oh. You did not come to see me. Hasn't your husband come to take you back?"

Sayantani was looking on in surprise.

Budni said, "My husband is dead. He hung himself with my saree. He doubted me. He wanted to know how my son was born only seven months after our marriage. He wanted to know how my son was so fair and handsome. My mother-in-law chased me out. I did not go back."

Snehamoy's face was burning. His conscience was shaken. He could no longer think straight.

Budni reached out for her son, kissed him and held him up joyfully to Snehamoy, "See, Babu, see how fair he is! Just like you."

Snehamoy started sweating in fear, but did not dare ask Budni to stop. How could he? The sun was illuminating the world, sending its rays far and wide. Darkness was powerless against the light.

Budni continued, "I have not used the bar of soap. The fault was not yours alone, Babu, but mine too. I have no sorrow, no grief. My son makes me forget everything with his heavenly smile. Here, hold my son, hold him just once."

Snehamoy's hands were trembling. Sayantani pushed him aside and came forward. "Give me your son. You have nothing to fear. Urangara has merged itself with Subarnarekha. And the sand of the riverbed has gold—that is the truth." Budni laughed; her eyes were brimming. The three of them stood there, looking at the child—so precious, so real, so beautiful.

Then, just as the river flows on to find its destination, each went their own way.

Translated by Anuradha Sen

Glossary

alta a red dye (originally produced from lac) used by Hindu women to paint their palms and feet

attar a perfume or essential oil extracted from flowers or petals, earlier widely used by courtesans and royalty

babughar an upper-caste household or residence

Banjaras an ancient nomadic ethnic community with disputed origins, a well-defined culture and oral traditions; also known variously as Gor Banjaras, Nayak and Lambadi, they are now distributed across much of India

Bene a sub-caste of goldsmiths in rural Bengal

bhagar a waste land, usually on the outskirts of a village or settlement, where dead bodies of animals are deposited

Birsa Munda iconic freedom fighter, tribal leader and folk hero of the Munda tribe who led an armed tribal rebellion against the British

boshtami fish a type of fish, commonly kept in tanks in Vaishnava temples, which thrive on parched rice

boubhat the ceremony in which a new bride serves food for the first time to her husband's kinsfolk

chutta a type of hand-rolled mini-cigar

deshi native or indigenous

dhaigiri the profession of a wet nurse and/or a midwife

dipti a corruption of the English word 'duty', mispronounced by the semi-literate security guard in the story

dodoma a double-sound firecracker, now banned

Dom a lower-caste community engaged in handling corpses and cremating the dead

Dwaparyug the third of the four yugas or ages in the Yuga Cycle according to the Hindu scriptures

ghagra-chunni a long, embroidered skirt worn with a veil or stole

Gour also Gauranga, another name of Chaitanya Mahaprabhu, a fifteenth-century Hindu mystic and Krishna devotee who had a profound influence on Vaishnavism in Bengal, and continues to have a strong presence in rural Bengal

haat an open-air rural market, commonly held on fixed days of the week, where farm produce, goods, services and livestock are traded

jaltaranga a melodic percussion instrument consisting of a set of ceramic bowls filled with water and played by striking the edges with beaters

jatra a folk theatre form popular in the Bengali-speaking areas of the Indian subcontinent

Jhumur an Indian folk dance form

jilipi jalebi; a wheel-shaped syrupy fried sweet

kadakhnocha a bird hunted for meat

Kaliyug the fourth yuga; the last stage of creation according to Hindu scriptures

kantha a handmade covering or thin blanket usually made from old sarees stitched together

Karma Puja worship of Karam Devta or the *karam* tree as deity, an important festival common to many tribal groups including the Santals, Mundas, Oraos, Hos and Kurmis, and celebrated across

	the states of Jharkhand, West Bengal, Madhya Pradesh, Chhattisgarh, Assam, Odisha and Bihar in India, and also Bangladesh
kartal	small hand cymbals used in pairs, normally consisting of round metal plates; used as accompaniment with devotional and folk songs
kendu	a major forest produce and important source of livelihood for Adivasi communities across India, leaves of the kendu tree are used to make bidis
khalasi	the helper of the driver of a vehicle, usually a truck or bus, who helps in the loading and unloading of goods and passengers
khichudi	a dish prepared by boiling rice and lentils together
khol	a two-sided terracotta drum used as accompanying percussion in devotional music
Khuro	a familiar or affectionate term meaning uncle
kolmi	an edible leaf popular in rural Bengal
kunda	star jasmine
mahua	Indian butter tree; also known as madhuka
Masi	aunt; here, used to refer to any elderly woman with social influence in the neighbourhood
paan	betel leaf
pardeshi	literally, 'from another land', an outsider, foreigner, non-native; here it refers to the foreign paddy seeds
parijan	literally, a close friend or family; here it refers to the palanquin
Phagun	the Bengali month of Phalgun which heralds spring and roughly corresponds with February/ March in the Gregorian calendar
prasad	food offered to a deity or the leftovers from a meal taken by a venerable superior
putush	lantana, a tropical flowering shrub

rajbhog	a syrupy sweet made of fresh cheese; a dessert similar to rasgulla
rakshasi	giantess; night-hag
sala	a slang term akin to 'scoundrel'
Sepoybabu	a generic form of address used for a policeman
shapla	water lily
shingi	a type of air-breathing catfish that has extra-respiratory organs or air sacs
shraddha	in Hinduism, ritual prayers and offerings made to the souls of departed ancestors, especially parents
Singbonga	the Sun god and supreme deity of the Mundas who saves the tribe from troubles
sukni	any dried, salted and seasoned fish
ukha	an indigenous, harp-like, stringed musical instrument used by tribal and folk minstrels
Urangara	a tributary of the river Subarnarekha
Yamraj	the god of death and king of the nether world in Hindu religious beliefs